Choosing to Finish Well

One
P.R.E.M.I.S.E.

ILYNMW Publishing
Atlanta Georgia

Dedication

This book is dedicated to my beautiful Bride and the love of my life - Debbie.   You are my best friend ever seen! Thanks for saying yes!

ISBN 978-0-9983413-2-3

Books by Paul Beersdorf

Flowers on Tuesday

52 Things I Wish My Father Had Told Me about Marriage and Family

The 100 Most Important Words

Encouraging Your Wife

Encouraging Your Husband

Advice for Today, Tomorrow and Forever

Even Moses Needed Encouragement

Storm Management

Living Intentionally

Contents

Acknowledgements

I love my Beautiful Bride and how much she encourages me to write and share my thoughts and ideas. She is the love of my life and my best friend. Nothing I do would be worthwhile without her by my side.

Preface

Several years ago, a dear friend of ours lost their mother after a long and difficult fight with cancer. She was an incredible woman who was dearly loved by many.

Predictably the funeral was packed with family and friends who wanted to offer their condolences and say goodbye to this wonderful woman. She had touched so many lives in a positive and meaningful way.

As the eulogy began there was a clear theme from all of the speakers. This was a woman who had lived a great life and had finished well. In fact, the last speaker – her youngest son used those very words to describe his mother. He said she had fought the good fight all her life and had finished well.

Those words have resonated with me since that day and I have long contemplated whether or not I would finish well. Then I had a bit of an epiphany and realized that finishing well is a choice and not luck or chance.

My choices, attitudes and actions would offer clear evidence as to whether I would finish well and I had 100% control over these. I know I am blessed to live in a country where I do have freedom and opportunity as well as the ability to make choices.

My heart's desire is that as you read this book, you will choose to take control of your life and choose to finish well. The choice really is yours!

Introduction

I am more than half way through my life, and I began to wonder what I was going to do with the rest of the time I had left on this earth? This is a common question for men and women who are at the mid-point of their life. One of my mentors suggested that I read the book Half-Time by Bob Buford. Since I am a big believer in continuing education and read 20-30 books per year, I added it to my reading list.

Since I typically read 5-7 books at a time, it took a while to work this book into my rotation. When I finally did work it into my reading list, I was so glad my mentor had suggested the book.

Even though I am well past half-time, the principles taught in the book are applicable to anybody. One of the key themes of the book is moving from success to significance. In other words, how was I going to spend the last half of my life? Was I going to be completely self-indulgent and partake in all the pleasures of retirement, or was I going to look for something more significant to do with my time, talents and treasures?

The huge ask from the book was – what was that ONE THING I was going to focus on in my life? It would be easier to create a list of the 100 things I was going to do with my life than to think of that ONE THING. What was most important? What was significant? What was most valuable? What was worthy of being that ONE THING?

As I thought and prayed about the ONE THING, it occurred to me that there were seven (7) key areas of my life that I wanted to refine and define and focus on one thing for each of those areas. They would all ultimately be driven by the ONE big THING.

These seven areas of life are true for everybody and are integrally linked together. You cannot focus on only one area without having an effect on another area. You have to be focused and dedicated to working on all seven areas of your life and ultimately defining the ONE THING for each of those areas. When you have done this you see how closely knit together they truly are – both now and in the future.

So what are the seven areas?

- Physically – your body and how your maintain it
- Relationally – how you deal with the people in your life
- Economically – how you manage your treasures
- Mentally – how you view circumstances
- Intellectually – your capacity to learn and use knowledge
- Spiritually –your relationship with God
- Emotionally – how you react to others

As I thought about these seven key areas of my life I wanted to distill this down to one word or phrase for each area. Not only would this make it easier for me to remember, but it would also make it easier for me to share with others. In business we would call this our "elevator speech". In other words, it can be done in about 15-30 seconds.

So here goes – I want to be:

Physically	– FIT
Relationally	– ENGAGED
Economically	- SOUND
Mentally	– POSITIVE
Intellectually	– CURIOUS
Spiritually	– GROUNDED
Emotionally	– SENSITIVE

Note the first letter of these key words spell out the acronym P.R.E.M.I.S.E. You will see this spelled out more fully in the next couple of chapters, but for now I just want you to know that I use this acronym because it is easy for me to remember and use when I share with others.

There are two other things to consider - my overall actions and attitude. My key action should be serving others and my attitude should be one of humility. These are two key pillars that will help me with my selfishness and prideful nature.

Underlying all of this is INTENTIONALITY!   This is my favorite word
these days.   I have determined to lead an intentional life and will do my
very best to be intentional about all that I say and do.   However, I will tell
you this is easier said than done! Intentionality takes hard work and
persistence.

Here is a picture of what that looks like for me:

I am a visual learner, so seeing this as a picture of a house helps me to
better understand and codify my goal of living a worthwhile life and
finishing well!

Now, when it comes to the ultimate **ONE THING**.

For me that is going to be serving God!   All of these other things will have to be subordinate to that ultimate ONE THING.   If I am successful in focusing on achieving the singular word that defines the ONE THING for each of these seven key areas of my life, while seeking to serve others with humility, then I believe I will draw closer to God.

It is my prayer that you will find your ONE THING and focus all of your time, talents and treasures on pursuing that ONE THING.

Two
Questions

Before you really get into this book, I have a few questions I want you to honestly answer.   We will come back to these answers later in the book, but it is important for you to take a little time before we start to answer these questions.

1. On average, how many hours do you spend in front of a screen each week (for pleasure not work)

- TV/Cable/Satellite
- Phone/Tablet
- Computer
- Gaming, Web Surfing, Social Media, Movies, etc.

Write your answer here: Avg. # of hours = _____

2. On average, and how much did you spend each month on the following?

- Fast Food (Chick-fil-a, McDonalds)
- Coffee/Beverage (Starbucks, Dunkin Donuts)
- Casual Dining or Fine (Applebee's, Outback)
- Hobbies?
- Movies, gaming, sports?
- Payments for Deprecating assets – boats, RV's, ATV's, motorcycles, snowmobiles, etc.

Write your answer here: Avg. amount spent = _____

Half-Time

Forty is the old age of youth; fifty is the youth of old age
- Victor Hugo

What is the significance of 28,413? This is the average number of days in your life! In the United States, the average life expectancy for Men is 76 and for Women it is 81 (the average being 78).

So if you are older than 40, then you are about half-way through your life! Worried? Don't be, the best years are ahead of you.

Here are 11 people who did some significant things after age 40.

George Mueller – Became a missionary at age 70

Sam Walton – founded Wal-Mart at age 44

Henry Ford – Introduced the Model T at age 45

Harland Sanders – started Kentucky Fried Chicken at age 62

Leo Goodwin – founded GEICO insurance at age 50

"Grandma" Moses – started painting at age 78

Ray Kroc – franchised McDonalds at age 52

Peter Roget – invented the Thesaurus at age 73

Moses – was 80 years old when he lead his people out of Egypt

Momofuku Ando – invented Ramen Noodles at age 48

Laura Ingles Wilder – started writing Little House on the Prairie at age 65

Age really is just a number. You can decide for yourself that the back half of your life will be more significant than the first half of your life.

As I am writing this chapter I have about 8,000 days left in my life (assuming I live to be 76 years old). I could look at this number and be dismayed by how little time I have left, or I can look at this number and be encouraged by how much time I have left.

As for me, I choose to have a significant second half of life. It is a choice! It is your choice. Remember the following: "To choose, not to choose, is to choose". You always have a choice.

I encourage you to take ownership of these statements:

- I choose to believe the best days are ahead of me and my family

- I choose to believe there is more to be learned.

- I choose to believe there is more to be taught and shared

- I choose to believe there are more people I can serve.

- I choose to have a positive outlook on the future.

- I choose to believe my time, talents and treasures can positively impact many people in the future.

- I choose to believe I can be a person of positive influence until my last breath.

If you sit back and do nothing, you have made your choice. I pray you will take the time to reflect on the first half of your life, and then focus on the back half of your life.

Start with reading Bob Buford's book *"Half-Time"*. This is a good starting point to change the trajectory of your second half.

As for me - I choose "Not to Go Gentle into that Good Night"

What will you choose?

Choices

To choose, not to choose, is to choose.
- Unknown

As I stated in the introduction, I came up with the acronym P.R.E.M.I.S.E., from the seven key areas of my life. It is an easy way for me to remember these seven key areas as well as share with others about how I am choosing to focus my energy and attention in the remaining day that I have to live and serve.

What is a PREMISE? It is a statement taken to be true and used as a basis for argument or reasoning.

Here is one of the more common definitions of a premise that helps people to understand the meaning.

- All humans are mortal.
- The president is a human.
- Therefore, the president is mortal.

So here is my PREMISE for this book.

PREMISE:

- Choices define how someone will live their life.
- We all have the ability to make choices.
- Therefore it is your choices that will define how you live your life..

While it is true that we get to make many choices each and every day, there are some things we do not get to choose.

What are some things you **<u>DID NOT</u>** get to choose?

- You did not get to choose your parents/family/siblings
- As a child you did not get to choose your environment or where you were born
- You did not get to choose your blood type
- You did not get to choose how tall the mountains would be, or the waters in the ocean, nor the stars in the sky
- You did not get to choose how others will act/react

Obviously there are other things you did not get to choose, however I would suggest the number of choices you do get to make vastly outnumber the choices you cannot make.

I have a friend at work that went to bed one night and woke up the next morning and could not walk! He had ruptured a disc in his back and was paralyzed from the waist down. That was six years ago, and he is one of the most joyful people you will ever meet. He will tell you that he did not choose to be paralyzed and in a wheelchair, but he can choose to have a positive attitude and be joyful. He chooses to focus on those things he can do, rather than those things he cannot do.

Let's think about this. What are some of the choices you made today?

What time to get up?
To answer your phone?
To bathe or not to bathe?
What to eat?
What to wear?
Where to sit?
Where to park?
To encourage someone?
What to ponder/think?
What to look at?
What to read?
To respond to that text, blog post, Facebook message or email?
Go to work, not go to work?
Take a nap or exercise?
Play a video game?
Make some repairs?
Practice your hobby?

This list could go on for pages and pages. We all make hundreds of choices each and every day. How many of those choices are intentional, thoughtful and productive? How many routine? How many are happenstance? Keep this in the back of your mind you read through this book.

I will challenge you to make some positive choices in your life. You can choose to make these choices or not, but know that you will be making a choice either way. The accountability and responsibility starts and stops with you. President Truman liked to say "The Buck Stops Here" – meaning he took full responsibility.

I urge you to carefully consider and pray about these choices. My prayer is that you would choose to take control of your life and no longer let obstacles (people, places, position, posture, time, resources) be the reason for not changing.

The choice is yours. The sooner you believe this, the sooner you can make positive change in your life.

Seven key choices I will ask you to make:

1. Will you choose to be physically fit?
2. Will you choose to be more engaged in your most important relationships?
3. Will you choose to lead an economically sound life?
4. Will you choose to be mentally positive?
5. Will you chose to be intellectually curious?
6. Will you choose to be spiritually grounded?
7. Will you choose to emotionally sensitive?

I have chosen to work towards these goals for the remainder of my life. For some of these it will be easy for me, for others it will be much more challenging. I am self-aware enough to realize my key areas of opportunity and know I will need help and accountability to fully realize my potential.

If you don't know which areas are most challenging for yourself, ask your family and friends to help you (and be prepared for their honest feedback – you may not appreciate it at first).

You have taken the first steps toward positive change by starting this book. Now let's continue the journey.

Some of you may not like the questions I will be challenging you with! I would ask you to be honest and truthful with your answers.

Shakespeare says it well in Hamlet:

"This above all: to thine own self be true"
Polonius (Hamlet Act 1, Scene III)

You have to honest with yourself and examine your life, motives, actions, thoughts, and devices.   And, oh by the way, you can hide nothing from God! So why kid yourself. Take the opportunity to look deep within and decide if you want to change the way you are going to lead your life.

Here is a great story I found at: *A Gift Of Inspiration.com*. The author is unknown

I woke up early today, excited over all I get to do before the clock strikes midnight. I have responsibilities to fulfill today and I am important. My job is to choose what kind of day I am going to have.

Today I can complain because the weather is rainy or I can be thankful that the grass is getting watered for free.

Today I can feel sad that I don't have more money or I can be glad that my finances encourage me to plan my purchases wisely and guide me away from waste.

Today I can grumble about my health or I can rejoice that I am alive.

Today I can lament over all that my parents didn't give me when I was growing up or I can feel grateful that they allowed me to be born.

Today I can cry because roses have thorns or I can celebrate that thorns have roses.

Today I can mourn my lack of friends or I can excitedly embark upon a quest to discover new relationships.

Today I can whine because I have to go to work or I can shout for joy because I have a job to do.

Today I can complain because I have to go to school or eagerly open my mind and fill it with rich new tidbits of knowledge.

Today I can murmur dejectedly because I have to do housework or I can appreciate that I have a place to call home.

Today stretches ahead of me, waiting to be shaped. And here I am, the sculptor who gets to do the shaping.

What today will be like is up to me. I get to choose what kind of day I will have!

Have a GREAT DAY ... unless you have other plans and please remember, a 'Smile' will make the days go better.

Source: http://agiftofinspiration.com.au/stories/attitude/Choices.shtml

Good Choices/Bad Choices

Let us look at two Bible characters that had the opportunity to make difficult choices. One of them made good choices and one of them made bad choices. Each choice clearly had serious consequences!

<u>Daniel</u>

In Daniel chapter 6, we find the familiar story of Daniel in the lion's den. Daniel had recently been promoted as one of three leaders in the kingdom and many other leaders were jealous of Daniel and wanted him removed.

They tried to find something against Daniel, but he was a righteous man and they could bring no charge against him. Therefore they appealed to the king's pride and had him create a law that would require everyone to worship the king as a god for 30 days. Anyone not doing that would be thrown in the lion's den.

In this way, they hoped to trap Daniel because they thought his strong believe in the GOD of Israel was his one weakness and they would use this against him to bring about his destruction.

In verse 10 we can see the clear choice that Daniel makes. Read below and study the words carefully:

Daniel 6:10

*Now when Daniel **knew** that the document was signed, he entered his house (now in his roof chamber he had windows open toward Jerusalem); and he continued kneeling on his knees three times a day, praying and giving thanks before his God, as he had been doing previously.*

Daniel knew what was coming. He KNEW the new law was being contemplated and he watched to see if it would actually be signed into law. As soon as he KNEW it was signed into law, he had a choice to make.

Would he continue to worship and praise the one true God or would he give into pressure, bow down to the king and keep his life?

He made a CHOICE to continue to worship in the way he had always worshipped. Openly and boldly! He chose to worship God and he chose to let those around him know about his choice. Not by bragging or talking about it, but by continuing to do what he had always done.

Of course we all know what happened next; he was thrown in the lion's den and then God delivered him from a certain death. Now many of us stop reading the story at that point, but if you continue to the end of the chapter we find that the king was so angry with Daniels accusers, he had all of them and their families (wife and children) thrown into the lion's den, where they all perished.

While we can see the clear choice that Daniel made, sometimes we miss the choice these other officials made. They chose to conspire against Daniel and create an unjust law to punish him. Unfortunately, their choice resulted in their death and the death of their family as well

Choices have consequences!

Daniel was prepared for the consequences and knew what he was doing. He was prepared because he continued to trust God, have faith, and be in prayer and study. Are you prepared for the challenges and choices that are coming your way? Choose to prepare by praying, studying, being in fellowship, seeking wisdom and discernment and seeking wise counsel.

David

King David, a man after God's own heart!   He was a man who wrote so many psalms and praised and worshiped God, and yet he was a man who made some rather poor choices.

In 2 Samuel chapters 11-12 we find the story of David and Bathsheba. In this story we find David making one bad choice after another.   In all, he makes three really bad choices.

Bad Choice #1 – It was the spring time and the kings sent their army off to war. It was the duty of the king to lead his army and be an example to his men. In this case, David stayed home and instead let Joab lead the army. David should have been with his army.

Bad Choice #2 – Now David was home with free time on his hands. His army was gone (and most of the fighting men).   He was distracted and not thinking about the battles and leading his country. Instead he sees a beautiful woman bathing on her roof top and decides he wants her. As the king he could do pretty much anything he wanted (including having sex with the wife of another man).

This woman we know is Bathsheba, and she becomes pregnant and tells the king.

Bad Choice #3 – David tries to hide his sin by sending for Bathsheba's husband – Uriah- (who was away doing battle for the kingdom) and hoping he would come home and sleep with his own wife and therefore believe he had made her pregnant.

When Uriah turned out to be a righteous man who would not go to his own house for a time of comfort and relaxation (because his men were suffering in the battle field), David decided to have Uriah killed.

He sent a note to Joab (by the hand of Uriah) and told Joab to place Uriah in the midst of the hardest fighting so that he might perish.

Indeed, Uriah died and then David took Bathsheba to be his wife. She had a son and everything seemed alright. But God's anger burned against David for the sin with Bathsheba and for the murder or Uriah. Therefore God sent the prophet Nathan to confront David.

In the end it was only tragedy. Uriah was killed (as were many others who had fought beside him), and the baby also died.

David's poor choices had lasting consequences for his life as well. See what Nathan has to tell David about the future of his household:

2 Samuel 12:10

Now therefore, the sword shall never depart from your house, because you have despised Me and have taken the wife of Uriah the Hittite to be your wife.'

Indeed, David had turmoil in his household for the rest of his days. It was very sad to see this Godly man make such poor choices. Nathan told him that what he had done in secret would be known publicly to everyone. To this day, this is a tragic tale the whole world knows.

I would encourage you to read Psalm 51. This was the Psalm that David wrote after this incident and it was his confession and plea for God to forgive him. It is a good example of reaching out to God at a low point and knowing that God can and will forgive.

This verse from Psalm 51:10 is probably familiar to you:

Psalm 51:10

Create in me a clean heart, O God,
And renew a steadfast spirit within me.

Finally, consider well the choices you will make in life and realize some of them will have everlasting consequences not only for you, but for your loved ones as well. Seek wisdom and wise counsel if you are not sure of your choices and try never to make a hasty decision.

The life you lead is a culmination of the choices you make each and every day. Choose to finish well – by making good choices!

Physically Fit

If we could give every individual the right amount of nourishment and exercise, not too little and not too much, we would have found the safest way to health.
- Hippocrates

A Football Story

What would happen if you wanted to play football but never did anything to prepare your body, heart and mind for that experience? Do you think you would enjoy spring training and "two-a-day" practices? How do you think your body would respond?   How would you feel in the heat of July and August in full pads hitting other players and spending 2 hours each day at practice?

These are all questions that were going through my mind as I thought about my son Jonathan and his desire to play football.

Caveat before we continue.   I never played football! I do not really even enjoy watching or attending football games (other than my son's games) and I went to the University of Alabama where football is a religion.   I just wanted to dissuade you of thinking I was some kind of football fanatic – I leave that to my Bride who is a football freak!   She loves the game.

With that out of the way we can continue.

My son Jonathan has talked about wanting to play football for some time now. His older brother played football and it just seemed like a good fit for him – given that he was a pretty big kid for his age. For various and sundry reasons we deferred this decision for several year.

When he turned 13 he suddenly got very serious and very persistent about wanting to play football. He and I had a discussion and I explained that playing football would require him to have a fitness level and discipline that heretofore, he did not possess.

You see, Jonathan was 5'8'', he weighed 180+ lbs. and to say he was "pudgy" would have been kind.

He and I had an honest conversation about what it would take for him to effectively play football and enjoy the game and have some level of success. I told him he would need the following:

- Strength
- Endurance/Stamina
- Speed

To be honest, he had none of these!

For strength, I told him he would need to be able to lift his own weight (because football is a very physical game and since he was one of the larger kids playing, if he could lift this weight, then he would be able to "move" other people around)

For endurance/stamina, I told him he would need to last for 4 full quarters. I told him that the team and players, who conditioned themselves to play for the entire game, would have a higher chance of being successful. I also told him, he would enjoy the practice and instruction time with the coaches if he was not fatigued.

For speed, I told him he would need to be able to attack and pursue the ball! Football is a game of speed.

We had this discussion in late December and we then put together a very intentional plan to get him to the point where he would be prepared for spring practice in April.

With everything in life, it is important to have a plan. If you fail to plan, they you should plan to fail.   I like to say "have a plan and work your plan".   If you want to succeed, you must be intentional and have a plan of action.

The Plan

Starting on January 2nd (the first Monday of the year), we did an assessment to gauge where his body was in terms of weight, strength and stamina. Spring training would start in late April, so we had about 15 weeks to change his trajectory from this staring point.

Here was his initial statistics:

Push Ups = 15
Sit Ups = 31
Bench Press = 80 lbs.
Running = none!

The assessment was very important, because we had to be honest with ourselves about his current condition and to also use this as a benchmark for improvement. How would we know if he improved if we did not measure against his starting point.

I will not go into all the details of the plan, but in summary it started very slowly and was methodical. His first week he only had to do 3 sets of 5 pushups and 3 sets of 10 crunches as well as some running – he did this 6 days a week. The idea was to start slow and develop routine and discipline.

By the time he got to spring training he had made significant progress!

Pushups = 61
Sit-ups = 72
Bench press 120 lbs.
Running = he could run for 30 minutes or just over 3 miles

He loved spring training!!   The workouts and training we did at home were much harder than anything they did at practice. He was able to listen and learn about the game and work on techniques that would serve him well when fall football started.

When spring was over, we laid out his "country boy" summer workout program.

It was designed to get him active and outdoors an also show him how to build muscles, strength and speed without being in a gym.

All summer long he had to do the following:

- Run 30 minutes first thing in the morning
- 15 sets of 10 pushups (150 pushups)
- 15 sets of 20 sit-ups (300 sit-ups)

Eat breakfast

Carry rocks (big huge rocks) up the hill from the creek in our backyard (about 200 meters). He spent an hour doing this each day.

Eat Lunch

Then from 6:00pm – 8:00 pm – he had to chop wood by hand with an axe. We had a huge oak tree that had fallen on the back of our property. I cut it into manageable pieces (about 6 feet long) with my chainsaw and then he spent the rest of the summer cutting those pieces into smaller pieces and them carrying each piece to our house (about 100 meters away).

The timing of doing this from 6:00pm to 8:00pm coincided with the exact timing of fall football practice.

To say he worked hard would be an understatement. He went through several sets of leather gloves that summer!

When he went back to fall football here are his results:

- Weight: 150 lbs. (solid as a rock)
- Pushups = 73
- Sit-ups = 87
- Bench Press = 160 lbs.
- Running = 3+ miles

What were the results?

He was the starting right guard on offense, the starting right tackle on defense; he started on special teams and basically played the entire game! This all happened for a kid who had never played a lick of football and really did not have any discernible athletic skills. It was all about having an intentional plan to be physically fit, following the plan, accountability, measuring progress and lots of encouragement.

We took before and after pictures and it is amazing to see the transformation he made.

This is not rocket science or new ideas. This is about intentionality and choice (attitude).

You may be asking yourself right now - what is the point of me sharing this story? Or, you may be saying to yourself- so what!

The point is this. We did all of this work just to prepare for a silly game called football. While this is fun, it is not nearly as important as preparing for the rest of your life!

How much more important is it for you to prepare yourself to serve your family, serve your job, serve your neighbors and community, serve others and to serve God? What if we put this much effort into taking care of our bodies so that we can be useful and productive? Football is just a game!

Questions

I want to start out each chapter by asking a series of questions. I will then end each chapter by asking a different set of questions. I will ask you to be honest with your answers and be truthful with yourself.

- Should we be physically fit?

- Are there benefits to being physically fit?

- Are there dangers/implications for not being physically fit?

My guess is that your answer to each of the questions above was "YES". This is pretty much common sense stuff when you get right down to it

Let's start with a great Bible verse about our bodies and how we should view taking care of our bodies from God's perspective.

1 Corinthians 6:19-20

Or do you not know that your body is a temple of the Holy Spirit who is in you, whom you have from God and that you are not your own for you have been bought with a price: therefore glorify God in your body.

Everything you will read in the chapters that follow is really common sense stuff. You have probably read or heard many of the ideas and concepts that I will present to you. Hopefully I will keep it simple and easy to follow. Too often we make the simple complicated and in reality this is not that difficult. This is mostly about choosing to make changes in your life that will positively impact you and those around you.

So, how can I be any earthly good if I have not taken care of my body???

If I am so out of shape that I cannot play with my children or grandchildren, do my job properly, work around the house or volunteer in my church or community, then I have effectively disqualified myself from serving others (much less taking care of myself).

Now I realize there are some of you who have debilitating conditions and illnesses that prevent you from being physically fit. This is certainly not directed at you. This is directed at the 98% of us who have no excuse – other than laziness or selfishness.

So when I say I want to be PHYSICALLY FIT, what does that mean? Well here is what it means to me in a nutshell:

1. Exercise – a healthy amount of exercise to lose and or maintain weight such that my body will be healthy and not obese or neglected
2. Eating & Drinking – to be very circumspect in what I putting into my body
3. Drugs – only those prescribed by a doctor and or OTC for common ailments (e.g. Ibuprofen)
4. Smoking – Never
5. Rest – get plenty of it

I know this may seem simplistic, but the truth is almost always very simple and common sense.

Ultimately, I want to be able to work and serve long into my "old age" (God willing) and the only way to do that is by being very intentional and proactive sooner in my life rather than later.

When I think of my physical body and being physically fit, it is all about wanting to be able to fulfill my mission and destiny in life to the best of my ability. I do not want to slink into the back half of my life in such bad shape that I could not even enjoy a beautiful day outside.

Let's start with the practical considerations for taking care of your body. Everybody knows that exercise and physical conditioning is good for you, but it is not enough to "know"! You have to actually put this into action and start a regular routine of exercise.

According to the CDC (Center for Disease Control) - Regular physical activity is one of the most important things you can do for your health. It can help:

- Control your weight
- Reduce your risk of cardiovascular disease
- Reduce your risk for type 2 diabetes and metabolic syndrome
- Reduce your risk of some cancers
- Strengthen your bones and muscles
- Improve your mental health and mood
- Improve your ability to do daily activities and prevent falls, if you're an older adult
- Increase your chances of living longer

https://www.cdc.gov/physicalactivity/basics/pa-health/index.htm

The Mayo clinic lists these other benefits to exercise:

- Exercise improves mood
- Exercise boosts energy
- Exercise promotes better sleep
- Exercise puts the spark back into your sex life
- Exercise can be fun … and social!

http://www.mayoclinic.org/healthy-lifestyle/fitness/in-depth/exercise/art-20048389

Two additional benefits of exercising:

- It is a positive example for your kids (and grandkids)
- To stay attractive for your spouse.

So let's think about this – you can live longer! Really? Yep! According to recent studies you can get a 7-1 return on exercise. In other words, for every minute of exercise you could gain 7 minutes in extended life. For a 40 year old this would add about 3.4 years to their life span. This assumes you follow the CDC exercise guidelines below.

http://commonhealth.legacy.wbur.org/2013/03/minutes-exercise-longer-life

So how much and how often should you exercise?

To be clear, these guidelines come for the CDC and are a good starting point. As always, you should consult with your doctor before beginning any exercise routine.

For Important Health Benefits - Adults need at least:

- 2 hours and 30 minutes (150 minutes) of moderate-intensity aerobic activity (i.e., brisk walking) every week and

- Weight training muscle-strengthening activities on 2 or more days a week that work all major muscle groups (legs, hips, back, abdomen, chest, shoulders, and arms).

OR

- 1 hour and 15 minutes (75 minutes) of vigorous-intensity aerobic activity (i.e., jogging or running) every week and

- muscle-strengthening activities on 2 or more days a week that work all major muscle groups (legs, hips, back, abdomen, chest, shoulders, and arms).

OR

- An equivalent mix of moderate- and vigorous-intensity aerobic activity and

- muscle-strengthening activities on 2 or more days a week that work all major muscle groups (legs, hips, back, abdomen, chest, shoulders, and arms).

https://www.cdc.gov/physicalactivity/basics/adults/index.htm

The CDC is probably one of the few government agencies that actually does a good job and provides a service to the tax payers of the United States. They have many free resources for you to use to help you along the way to a healthier life style. The website below is a good starting point.

https://health.gov/paguidelines/guidelines/

So it is not just enough to know about exercise, it is up to you to put the wheels in motion to start exercising.

So you may want to know: - What do I do for exercise? Great question! Here is a sample week of my exercise plan

- When? Get up early(5:00 am) to have time to get in my exercise
- Frequency? 6 days per week (I rest on Sunday)
- Where? Home or Gym
- How: 45 minutes of calisthenics (pushups and or core body work) or weight lifting
- How: 45-60 minutes of aerobic exercise
- That is a total of about 9 hours of exercise per week

(note: I have been doing this for a long time, so do not think this is your starting point. Start slow and check with your doctor before beginning any new exercise routine)

I will tell you that this is not easy at all, but it is necessary. There are 168 hours in each week and I am allocating about 5.0% of my time each week to exercise (this of course does not include driving time, stretching, warming up, cooling down and cleaning up). If I add in all of these other activities that go along with exercise, then I am up to about 10.0% of my time each week.

You have to choose to begin an exercise routine and be intentional each week about completing the work.

Now, I am only going to briefly touch on the subject of eating and drinking. There are tons of great resources on what to eat and drink and proper diet and nutrition, but I will offer some of the simple and common sense things most of us already know, but needed to be reminded of and put into practice.

Drinking

- Drink more water
- Limit your drinks that have calories
- Limit your drinks with caffeine
- Do not consume alcoholic beverages

Eating

- Eat more fruits and vegetables
- Eat out less – cook more meals at home (using fresh food)
- Eat less processed food and less sugar
- Eat less/exercise more
- Don't skip meals
- Eat slower

Smoking

- Don't smoke!

Rest

The national sleep foundation suggest the following hours of sleep:

- Younger adults (18-25): Sleep range is 7-9 hours
- Adults (26-64): Sleep range did not change and remains 7-9 hours
- Older adults (65+): Sleep range is 7-8 hours

Like I said at the beginning of this chapter, this is not rocket science. It is common sense and self-discipline. You can choose to take control of this aspect of your life. It is a choice! It is your choice.

Romans 12:1

Therefore I urge you, brethren, by the mercies of God, to present your bodies a living and holy sacrifice, acceptable to God, which is your spiritual service of worship.

God desires us to take care of our body and be useful now and into the future.

Perspective

I also want to offer another perspective on exercise and being physically fit. When Paul was talking to Timothy he told him the following in regards to being physically fit:

1 Timothy 4:8

for bodily discipline is only of little profit, but godliness is profitable for all things, since it holds promise for the present life and also for the life to come.

God is most concerned about our spiritually fitness and godliness (we will talk about this later). The condition of our heart is most important to God.

Consider what God said to Samuel as he was looking for the next king of Israel. God had rejected Saul as king of Israel. Saul was a large man and clearly "looked" like a king. But God considered his heart and knew he was not the man to lead Israel.

Therefore, Samuel went to the house of Jesse to consider his many different sons'. Samuel was impressed with their outward appearance, but God wanted him to look deeper. See what God says to Samuel as the first son of Jesse is brought forward.

1 Samuel 16:7

But the Lord said to Samuel, "Do not look at his appearance or at the height of his stature, because I have rejected him; for God sees not as man sees, for man looks at the outward appearance, but the Lord looks at the heart."

And so it continued with the seven oldest sons of Jesse. Each one of them was rejected. Until David was called from his flock to be anointed king.

It is often said you should not judge a book by its cover!

Know that God is most concerned with the condition of your heart and your head (mind). Being physically fit will allow you to be used by God to fulfill your purpose and achieve all the goals and objective towards finishing well.

Choose today to be physically fit.

<u>Tough Questions:</u>

These questions are a bit tougher and you may not appreciate me asking. However, please be honest with your answers and with yourself. You are the one who is going to benefit

- Would your family and friends say you were physically fit?

- Do you think you are physically fit?

- If you are not physically fit – why not?

- What is holding you back? Is it time, mental, physical, emotional, or financial reasons that are holding you back? Are these real obstacles?

Lack of activity destroys the good condition of every human being, while movement and methodical physical exercise save it and preserve it.
-Plato

Relationally Engaged

Do you have the ability to focus on a singular task? Can you zone out and tune out everything and zero in on a problem? To my own detriment, I have this capability. While this is very useful at times (especially at work), it can also cause me to lose focus on people, and people are more important than tasks.

Recently I was working on this book and the accompanying Sunday School lesson I was preparing. I had 41 pages of notes and needed to get it down to a much more reasonable number to share with my class. It was Saturday evening and I would be teaching in the morning. I still needed to practice my lesson and put the finishing touches on it.

I was in my basement office and I had my music going (which is a signal to my family that I am working and focused on a task). Several hours had passed and I had not come up for air. I totally missed that my youngest daughter had just gotten home from her job at Chick-fil-a. She had worked a 9 hour shift and was exhausted, but she had also had a very bad experience with a customer and needed to talk.

She came bounding down the steps to my office and tentatively opened the door. I looked up from my computer and could see she was anxious to talk. I had a choice to make at that very moment. Here I was writing a lesson and a book about engaging people in relationships and I was HYPER FOCUSED on completing my Sunday School lesson.

What was I going to do?

I choose to do the right thing! I closed my lap top, pointed her to a seat and opened my ears and my heart to my beautiful daughter. Words poured out of her for 45 minutes (she really needed to talk). I asked only a few questions and let her ramble on about her day and this horrible customer experience she had to deal with.

It was very late in the evening when she was finished and I left my lesson and book on my desk. I knew I could get up early in the morning and finish up my work and in the end, she was more important than the task I was trying to complete.

I have to be honest and tell you that this was not a natural choice for me. I had to intentionally choose to make that time for my daughter in that moment. My "natural" inclination is to tell her I am busy and I will talk to here when I have a chance. However, since I have started on this intentional journey to be more engaged with these important relationships in my life I am very focused on doing the right thing and making better choices on how to spend my time.

Questions

1. What does it mean to be relationally engaged?

2. Should we be more engaged in our relationships?

3. What are the benefits of being more engaged?

4. What causes us to not be relationally engaged?

What does it mean to be relationally engaged?

Being relationally engaged means you are investing the right amount of time, energy and effort in the most important relationships in your life. It means you are there in the movement when someone is talking to you. It means you take the time to listen and encourage.

Being relationally engaged is a contact sport. It is not passive, it is active and alive. It means you have to focus and be intentional. You cannot drift or wander. You must choose to be relationally engaged.

Should we be more engaged in our relationships?

Of course we should be more engaged in our most important relationships. Not only will this benefit us, it will benefit others as well. It has been said that "no man is an island". Meaning, we were not meant to roam the earth alone. God designed us to be social creatures that belong to a family and a community.

Consider that the Bible tells us in 1 Corinthians chapter 12 that we are the body of Christ. Each of us has a different and unique purpose. Some are the eyes, others the hands, some the feet, and so forth. One member of the body cannot exist without the other parts of the body. All of the body parts are meant to work together. Therefore, all of the body parts have to be engaged and working together to fulfill their ultimate purpose.

Benefits of being relationally engaged:

According to Harvard Medical School, having strong and healthy relationships with family, friends and community have several key benefits:

- People are happier
- Have fewer health problems
- They live longer lives

Conversely, they also found that not having strong relationships increased the risk of death from all causes my 50%. So it is safe to say there are some pretty strong mental and physical benefits to having strong relationships.

What about other benefits? If you have strong relationships and are more engaged you can:

- Encourage others
- Be encouraged
- Have accountability
- Have prayer partners
- More meaningful Bible study and fellowship
- More meaningful worship and praise
- People to walk through the valley and experience the mountain top moments of life

Ecclesiastes 4:9-12

Two are better than one because they have a good return for their labor. For if either of them falls, the one will lift up his companion. But woe to the one who falls when there is not another to lift him up. Furthermore, if two lie down together they keep warm, but how can one be warm alone? And if one can overpower him who is alone, two can resist him. A cord of three strands is not quickly torn apart.

What causes us to not be relationally engaged?

It was very easy for me to come up with this list, because I am much too familiar with each of these reasons. I have been guilty at one time or another of employing each of these, much to the detriment of my closest relationships.

Here are some of the main causes that keep us from being relationally engaged?

1. Selfishness – we want to spend our time energy and effort on ourselves and our own wants, needs and desires. We are not tuned into the needs of others.
2. Hard heart – lack of sympathy/empathy – we just don't care!
3. Busyness – we get so wound up in all kinds of things that on the surface seem important, but in the end just take up more time. Joining another committee, attending another meeting, never saying no when someone asks for assistance.
4. Distractions – cell phone, internet, TV, games, sports, hobbies, work, career, ministry! Yes ministry. We can work so hard at meeting the needs of others, that we neglect the most important relationships in our life.
5. Lack of planning – if you fail to plan, plan to fail. You have to know how you will use your time, so you can wisely spend it with the most important people in your life.
6. Laziness – not willing to work hard and make sacrifices

Do any of these resonate with you? Can you see how some or all of these are causing you to not be fully engaged in those most important relationship?

The choice is yours to change how you will be engaged (or not).

What choices do you make when it comes to being relationally engaged?

Physically – will you choose to be present and available?

Mentally – will you choose to be there mentally?   Will you choose to listen and pay attention?

Emotionally – will you choose to be empathetic and or sympathetic?

Spiritually – will you choose to pray, praise, fellowship, worship, hold accountable, encourage and be there for others?

Time – will you choose to allocate the proper amount of time to develop and grow these relationships?

It is your choice.   You get to choose whether or not you are going to be relationally engaged or not.   Will it take time, energy and effort? It sure will. Is it worth the time, energy and effort? It sure is!

Will there be times when others will disappoint your, treat you badly, ignore you or cause you pain and discomfort. Yes of course this will happen. But guess what, you do not always get to choose the circumstances, but you can always choose your response.   Stop worrying about what others are doing or not doing and choose what you are going to do. You have 100% control over that.

What are some of the relationships we are dealing with each day?

Beside each one I put the one word I want to be associated with that relationship. This is what I will strive for in each relationship.

- **Spouse** - Faithful
- **Children** – Teacher
- **Extended Family-** Provider/Protector
- **Employee** - Diligent
- **Friends** - Loyal
- **Neighbors** – Respectful
- **Fellow Believers** - Loving
- **Strangers** - Hospitality
- **Enemies** - Kindness

Spouse - Faithful

Proverbs 5:15

Drink water from your own cistern
And fresh water from your own well.

The divorce rate in America is about 50%. I do not desire to become part of that statistic. In the verse above Solomon is using a saying that would be very well known to the reader of that day.

In a dry and arid region, water is everything! It is literally life itself. Nothing can survive without water. A cistern (or well) would be dug by man for himself and his livestock. It was his well and his alone. Others were not allowed to use the well or drink from it.

The Bible commentaries tell us that this allegorical statement (fancy way of saying symbolic) is about marriage and fidelity within that marriage. The well is your Bride and the fresh water is the pure and enjoyable intimacy you share with your Bride and her alone!

So my desire is for my Bride and her alone. In other words, I need to be faithful to her in action, thought and deed. In a culture today that tells us to do whatever we want, with whomever we want, whenever we want, you have to choose to be faithful and honor your marriage!

Hebrews 13:4

Marriage is to be held in honor among all, and the marriage bed is to be undefiled; for fornicators and adulterers God will judge.

Ephesians 5:25

Husbands, love your wives, just as Christ also loved the church and gave Himself up for her,

Proverbs 5:18

Let your fountain be blessed,
And rejoice in the wife of your youth

Children – Teacher

How do children spell LOVE? They spell it - TIME

I have four children – two boys and two girls. Ages right now, 25, 24, 16 & 14. I have been doing this parenting thing for 25 years now and I can tell you one undeniable truth……. I don't have it all figured out yet. If you hear from any "expert" who tells you they have figured it all out, I would be very skeptical.

With that said, I do know that my primary function as parent is to teach my children. Even with my 25 year old daughter, there are still so many life lessons to teach her as she goes through different stages of her life and career. I have figured out that my teaching will only end, when I take my last breath and depart this earth.

Read the two verses below and commit them to your heart and memory! Do not neglect to teach your children, nor should you subcontract out the teaching of your children to others. You need to choose to be the primary teacher to your children. In all things! Here are seven key areas to teach your children. See if these look familiar:

- Physical fitness
- Relationships
- Economics and money management
- Mental attitude, actions and consequences
- Intellectual growth, education and learning
- Spiritual growth
- Emotional intelligence

Proverbs 22:6
Train up a child in the way he should go,
Even when he is old he will not depart from it.

Deuteronomy 6:6-9

These words, which I am commanding you today, shall be on your heart. You shall teach them diligently to your sons and shall talk of them when you sit in your house and when you walk by the way and when you lie down and when you rise up. You shall bind them as a sign on your hand and they shall be as frontals on your forehead. You shall write them on the doorposts of your house and on your gates.

Extended Family- Provider/Protector

1 Timothy 5:8

But if anyone does not provide for his own, and especially for those of his household, he has denied the faith and is worse than an unbeliever.

Chose to be the provider and protector for your immediate and extended family.   Choose to look beyond your own selfish nature and choose to serve your family first and foremost.   Yes we want to help others, but we must not neglect our family in the pursuit of helping others.

"The light that shines farthest shines brightest nearest home"
C.T. Studd

Employee - Diligent

Being diligent in the work place means showing up and doing your job. My grandfather used to tell me, "at the end day, you should owe your employer nothing more than they deserve and they should owe you nothing less than you have earned".

A fair day's work for a fair day's wage.   You are both even at the end of each day.

Floating around the internet is this list of 10 things that require ZERO talent.   While it can be argued that many of these are skills learned over time, it is clear everybody has the opportunity (and choice) to exhibit these characteristics in the work place.

1. Being on time
2. Work Ethic
3. Effort
4. Body language
5. Energy (Motivation)
6. Attitude
7. Passion
8. Being coachable
9. Doing extra
10. Being prepared

Opportunity is missed by most people because it is dressed in overalls and looks like work. --Thomas Edison

*I'm a great believer in luck, and I find the harder I work the more I have of it. --*Thomas Jefferson

It is your choice whether or not you will be a diligent worker or not. Each day you arise and have to choose what you will or will not do on the job. Remember, we are called to do our work for the Lord as opposed to doing it for men. We are called to consider the lowly ant that has no master at all, and yet the ant works diligently to prepare and provide. Are we not better than ants? God has given us a keen mind; body and spirit so we can work hard and do our very best.

Also, this same principle applies to the student as well as someone who is only working from home. Diligence is a full time job! Choose to be diligent in all your work.

Colossians 3:23

Whatever you do, do your work heartily, as for the Lord rather than for men,

Proverbs 14:23

In all labor there is profit,
But mere talk leads only to poverty.

Proverbs 6:6-11

Go to the ant, O sluggard,
Observe her ways and be wise,
Which, having no chief,
Officer or ruler,
Prepares her food in the summer
And gathers her provision in the harvest.
How long will you lie down, O sluggard?
When will you arise from your sleep?
"A little sleep, a little slumber,
A little folding of the hands to rest" –
Your poverty will come in like a vagabond
And your need like an armed man.

Friends - Loyal

It is imperative to concentrate on a few key friendships; I call those the 3am phone call friends. Those are the friends you will call at 3am when you are in great distress. You know they will be there by your side, no matter what happens. In other words, loyal friendships.

We all have many acquaintances and people we know, but at the end of the day if you walk out of this life with just a handful for real friends, you will have been blessed.

Real friendship is hard work. It is hard, because real friends have to be truthful sometimes, even when it can be hurtful. However, when done with love and tenderness; it can help restore a friend who has fallen away.

If you have a lot of friends, I would encourage you to choose a few of these relationships that you really want to dive into and develop even more. Choose to make the investment of time, talents and treasures to build up these friendships and create meaningful bonds that will not break no matter how difficult the storm.

Consider the verses below as you think about building lasting friendships.

Proverbs 17:17

A friend loves at all times,
And a brother is born for adversity.

Proverbs 18:24

A man of too many friends comes to ruin,
But there is a friend who sticks closer than a brother

Ecclesiastes 4:9-10

Two are better than one because they have a good return for their labor. For if either of them falls, the one will lift up his companion. But woe to the one who falls when there is not another to lift him up.

if you have not done so already, choose today who you want to be your 3am friends,

Neighbors – Respectful

Neighbors are mentioned in the Bible more than 130 times. Jesus was asked by the lawyer "who is my neighbor" and Jesus went on to tell the parable about the Good Samaritan.

So why should we be concerned about our neighbors? Because it is the second greatest commandment in the Bible! See what Jesus says below:

Mark 12:31

The second is this, 'You shall love your neighbor as yourself.'

We have to choose to be respectful of our neighbor. If we borrow something, we return it better than we received it. It we break something, we replace it. If our neighbor needs help or is hurting, we are there to lend an open hand and an open heart.

We respect their rights, their property, their family and their feelings. Even if they do not reciprocate! Especially if they do not reciprocate. Just because they are not good neighbors, does not give us a "pass" on being a good neighbor.

You have to choose to be a good neighbor and choose to love and serve them.

Read the key verses below on our relationship with our neighbors.

Romans 13:10

Love does no wrong to a neighbor; therefore love is the fulfillment of the law.

Romans 15:2

Each of us is to please his neighbor for his good, to his edification.

Proverbs 3:29

Do not devise harm against your neighbor,
While he lives securely beside you.

Fellow Believers - Loving

There is so much I could write about my relationship with my fellow believers, but to keep it simple I want to be loving towards them. Jesus tells us about a "NEW COMMANDANT", that we love one another.

What does love look like in the context of fellow believers? It looks like an action. Here are some of the ways we show love to our fellow believers:

- Praying for them
- Praying with them
- Caring for them when they are sick or hurting
- Meeting their financial needs in times of crisis
- Worshiping with them
- Encouraging them
- Coming along side and helping them with basics of life (moving, child care, cleaning, etc.)
- Sharing together
- Breaking bread together
- At times – admonishing them

Why is love so important?

If you read 1 Corinthians 13 (this is the "love chapter" of the Bible"), you can see how important love is to the equation of relationships.

Love is a choice and I hope you choose to love your fellow believer.

John 13:34

A new commandment I give to you, that you love one another, even as I have loved you, that you also love one another.

1 Corinthians 13

If I speak with the tongues of men and of angels, but do not have love, I have become a noisy gong or a clanging cymbal. If I have the gift of prophecy, and know all mysteries and all knowledge; and if I have all faith, so as to remove mountains, but do not have love, I am nothing. And if I give all my possessions to feed the poor, and if I surrender my body to be burned, but do not have love, it profits me nothing.

Love is patient, love is kind and is not jealous; love does not brag and is not arrogant, does not act unbecomingly; it does not seek its own, is not provoked, does not take into account a wrong suffered, does not rejoice in unrighteousness, but rejoices with the truth; bears all things, believes all things, hopes all things, endures all things.

Love never fails; but if there are gifts of prophecy, they will be done away; if there are tongues, they will cease; if there is knowledge, it will be done away. For we know in part and we prophesy in part; but when the perfect comes, the partial will be done away. When I was a child, I used to speak like a child, think like a child, reason like a child; when I became a man, I did away with childish things. For now we see in a mirror dimly, but then face to face; now I know in part, but then I will know fully just as I also have been fully known. But now faith, hope, love, abide these three; but the greatest of these is love.

Strangers - Hospitality

Showing hospitality comes easily to some people. I have to admit this has been difficult for me in the past. I have to intentionally choose to show hospitality towards strangers. It is not a natural inclination that I have. My beautiful Bride is much more accommodating than I and I know it is an area of opportunity for me to improve upon.

I love camping and in north Georgia we have the largest National Wilderness Area east of the Mississippi River, less than an hour from my front door. It is a glorious place to camp and hike and get away from "civilization" for a while.

A wilderness area by definition is remote. To get to our camp ground we have to take forest service roads (read single lane gravel road) up a very steep path. This is definitely not for the uninitiated. There are no houses, stores, building or anything in this remote location, which make it both glorious if you like solitude, but treacherous if you need help.

My son Jonathan and I headed up for a weekend of camping before the site closed at the end of October. If we did not get this last trip in, then we would have to wait until Mid-April to go again.

In short, we had a great weekend that started with clear sky and temperatures in the 70's on Friday, to a rainy and very windy Saturday in the 40's and then to our surprise – snow and temperatures in the 20's! We were well prepared for the cold and rain and had a good time in spite of the conditions.

After we had packed up on Sunday morning, we headed out for the slow drive home on the frozen forest service roads. There were few people out that weekend as they we smarter than us and decided to avoid the cold and wet weather (I think all weather is good camping weather – except for extreme heat and humidity).

As we were slowly making our way back, I noticed some people off the beaten path in a little used camping area. I commented to my son that it was an unusual place to camp. He told me to pay better attention as he thought the man was waving to us and needed some help.

Sure enough, I looked in my rear view mirror and I could see him frantically waving to us. I stopped the van and started to look for a place to turn around. This is not easily done on these narrow roads that have steep drop offs.

When we finally turned the van around, we got to the man (his name was Chris) and he asked if we could jump his Land Cruiser off. It seemed the battery had died in the cold weather.

We tried for 15-20 minutes to jump him off, but nothing seemed to work. It was freezing outside and his girlfriend was in the truck shivering from the cold.

I asked Chris what he would like to do at this point. He was new to camping in the area and I had been there dozens of times. I told him that town was only 20 miles away (about a 45 minute drive on these roads) and we would be happy to unload our van and put all of them in and take them down the mountain.

He talked to his girlfriend and they declined. He had just called his buddy and he said his friend would be there in 4-5 hours to tow them out. I asked how they would keep warm (as they could not use the heater in his truck).

Chris said they had good sleeping bags, they would put their tent back up and then wait for their friend. Having camped in the cold many times, being confined to a sleeping bag at night is misery enough, let alone having to do it during the day.

I then offered him my entire stash of fleece blankets (we had four of them) as well as my space heater and all the gas canisters I had left. This was more than enough gas to run the heater all day and night if necessary. It would make the wait much more tolerant if not pleasant.

He gladly took me up on my offer and I could sense the relief he felt. He wanted my cell number so he could figure out how to send my stuff back to me and I told him we would worry about that later (in my mind I had already decided to let him keep everything and let him pay it forward one day to someone else). I told him that people were more important than possessions and it was people who mattered and not stuff.

I took the opportunity to tell him about this book and the journey I was on to finish well. I told him that one of the things I wrote about was taking care of strangers and being a blessing to them. I told him to look upon this as a great adventure and that God was watching over him.

The next day, Chris did call me and told me of the adventure and how they finally got down the mountain. I was relieved that they were safe and sound. He thanked me profusely and asked how he could get my stuff back to me and as planned I told him to keep everything and "pay it forward" to someone else. I asked him to thank God each time they had the opportunity to use the blankets or heater and to tell others of God's grace, mercy and provision.

Chris was so thankful to God and for all the people who helped him that day. He said he saw clearly how God orchestrated all of the people to help them and get them to where they needed to be. God received the honor and glory and that is how it should be!

Not only did we create a positive experience for Chris, but I also set a good example for my son Jonathan. He was able to see my actions and not just my words. I have been a dad long enough to know that kids will ultimately follow you example before they follow what you say.

If you see someone in distress, take the time to leave your agenda and choose to meet their needs. You just might make a lifelong memory.

BTW – I asked Chris's permission to share this story.   He readily agreed!

What will you choose to do when you are encountered with strangers in need of food, clothing or shelter? It is a choice! Will you turn your back, or open your heart and your home?

Hebrews 13:2

Do not neglect to show hospitality to strangers, for by this some have entertained angels without knowing it.

Exodus 22:21

"You shall not wrong a stranger or oppress him, for you were strangers in the land of Egypt.

Matthew 25:35-40

For I was hungry, and you gave Me something to eat; I was thirsty, and you gave Me something to drink; I was a stranger, and you invited Me in; naked, and you clothed Me; I was sick, and you visited Me; I was in prison, and you came to Me.' Then the righteous will answer Him, 'Lord, when did we see You hungry, and feed You, or thirsty, and give You something to drink? And when did we see You a stranger, and invite You in, or naked, and clothe You? When did we see You sick, or in prison, and come to You?' The King will answer and say to them, 'Truly I say to you, to the extent that you did it to one of these brothers of Mine, even the least of them, you did it to Me.'

Take the opportunity this week to notice stranger around you who might need help or comfort.   If you open your eyes and if you are very intentional, you will see more people who need help than you think.

Strangers you might see:

- Homeless person on corner – don't give them money, but perhaps buy them a meal or give them some food.

- Person on side of road in broken down car – stop and offer assistance.

- Someone at a store struggling to put purchases in their vehicle

Enemies - Kindness

Show kindness to our enemies? That is crazy talk. Or is it?

The Bible teaches us to be at peace with all men (if it is within our means to do so). God desires us to have no enemies, and yet we know that because of the evil in the world, we will have enemies.

We are called to love our enemies and in doing so it will be like heaping burning coals on their head. Now that sounds like a plan! Sign me up to heap the burning coals on their heads. I did not fully understand this until I did some research.

To heap burning coals on the head or our enemies is about having them show contrition and look for forgiveness for their past wrongs and sins. It refers to the Egyptian principle of a person walking through town with a bowl of coals on their head as an acknowledgement of their repentance for their sins and an outward sign to the community that they are sorry and want to change.

You see God's desire to bring everybody back into a loving relationship with Himself and he can use us as an instrument to bring even our enemies to a point of repentance and change by showing love and kindness.

This is much easier said than done and it is a choice for us to believe and trust God to give us this love and kindness to show to our enemies. In our own strength and intellect this would be impossible! But with God, all things are possible.
Will you choose to love your enemies and show them kindness?

A few years ago, I had the opportunity to put my faith to the test in this area of my life.

When I joined a new work group, to say that I was an outsider would be the understatement of the year. The group was characterized by hard drinking and parties while away on business meeting. Since this was not my "cup of tea", I would usually excuse myself and head back to my room each night.

After one particularly long meeting, I headed home to my family. A few days later I received a phone call from a good friend.

He warned me to "watch my back" with this group of people. He then related a story about a man named Howard (not his real name) who had many derogatory things to say about me behind my back. Nobody defended me and others joined in with comments of their own. Howard clearly had it out for me and wanted to see me vanish from the team.

I related this story to my Bride and to say I was a little angry would not do justice to the way I really felt. I "stewed" over this situation and looked forward to a face to face encounter with Howard (He lives in a different state and we only see each other at the group meetings) so that I could relate to him my true feeling. I was looking for confrontation.

However, God got a hold of my heart and really spoke to me about my attitude and anger. My Bride was also a great blessing and counselor.

We had a team meeting out West and Debbie would be joining me. Debbie and I talked about Howard and how I should treat him. We decided to "kill him with kindness". I prayed for an opportunity to show kindness to him.

God in His wisdom gave me two such opportunities.

On the first day of our meeting, Debbie and I were eating breakfast and who should walk in but Howard.

I got up and asked him to come over and meet my Bride. I then proceeded to tell her about the recent business success that Howard had had and also congratulate him on the successful completion of his MBA. He grinned from ear to ear and I could see that he was very proud of his accomplishments (as he should be).

After he left, I looked at my Bride and she gave me the approving look and smile that only a proud wife can. She told me that I had handled that very well and she was proud of me.

The next incident came a day later.

We were staying at a resort that was at 9,500 feet. Many people got altitude sickness. I had gotten a double prescription of altitude sickness pills for Debbie and myself, but I decided that I would not take the medication unless I became symptomatic.

Guess who got altitude sickness? That's right, Howard. Guess who did not have any medication? That's right, Howard.

I went to Howard and told him that I would share my medication with him and he was very very grateful. Howard missed the first part of our meeting, but with help from the medication, he was back the next day.

The following day, I had the opportunity to give an impromptu presentation to our group. We had an instructor at the meeting who was teaching us about presentation skills and I had volunteered to go first. Somebody in the audience got to pick a subject (one that I did not know anything about) and I had to give a presentation to the group. Through God's grace and mercy I was able to do a good job.

When the instructor asked for feedback from the group, the first person to speak up was Howard. I was still standing in front of the room and did not know what to expect. The words of praise and admiration that came from him were incredible. It was like water for a man who had been walking through the desert for days. It provided both a physical and mental relief and fulfillment.

While showing kindness was not my first instinct or thought, it was absolutely the right thing to do. God proved faithful!

God is so good all the time!

Romans 12:18

If possible, so far as it depends on you, be at peace with all men

Luke 6:35

*But love your enemies, and do good, and lend, expecting nothing in return; and your reward will be great, and you will be sons of the Most High; for He Himself is **kind** to ungrateful and evil men.*

Proverbs 24:17

Do not rejoice when your enemy falls,
And do not let your heart be glad when he stumbles;

Luke 6:27-28

"But I say to you who hear, love your enemies, do good to those who hate you,
bless those who curse you, pray for those who mistreat you.

Romans 12:20

"But if your enemy is hungry, feed him, and if he is thirsty, give him a drink; for
in so doing you will heap burning coals on his head."

Proverbs 25:21-22

If your enemy is hungry, give him food to eat;
And if he is thirsty, give him water to drink;
For you will heap burning coals on his head,
And the Lord will reward you.

Tough Questions:

- Are you fully engaged with the most important relationships in your life?

- If not, why not? What is holding you back?

- Would your family and friends say you were fully engaged?

- Which relationship is hardest for you? Why?

- How hard are you willing to work to restore a relationship?

Economically Sound

Too many people spend money they earned, to buy things they don't want, to impress people that they don't like. --Will Rogers

Money and finances are two of the key issues that individuals and families struggle with. These issues can cause strife and discord if not properly managed.

Think about your own life. Can you point to times in your life when you and your family struggled with money and possessions? Perhaps that time is right now.

I recently read an article that said over ½ of Americans would have difficulty coming up with $500 for an emergency expense. If your savings account balance is hovering at or below $1,000, you're not alone.

According to a 2017 GOBankingRates.com survey, more than half of Americans have less than $1,000 in their savings accounts. Amazingly, 39% have ZERO money saved.

How important is it to be economically sound? The Bible has about 500 verses on prayer, about 500 verses on faith, but more than 2,000 verses on money and possessions. Money and possessions are a universal subject no matter what your background, religion or area of the world you live in.

So, what do I mean by economically sound? It is simply this: To be a good steward of your financial resources and use them to serve your family and others.

Questions

- Should you be a good steward of your financial resources?

- Should you save more?

- Should you spend less?

- Should you be more generous?

- Should you have a budget and follow it?

- Are there serious implications for not being economically sound?

Did you answer "YES" to all of those questions? I hope so.

Let me explain how we are trying to be economically sound in our marriage. It is very simple principles that have been around for a long time. None of these ideas are new. They are practical and work if you follow them diligently.

Here they are:

- Don't spend more than you make
- Save more
- Spend Less
- No debt (except for home mortgage)
- Pay cash (or debit card)
- Be generous

You probably look at this list and say "wow, that's it"? Yep, like I said, it is a very simple list. But remember, it is not enough to know, you have to be willing to act and take the right steps to be economically sound.

So why do I want to be Economically Sound? Here is my one simple reason: Peace of mind

Peace of Mind

When debt is looming over you, you become a virtual slave to the lender. It permeates every aspect of your life and creates friction in all of your key relationships.   You worry about what bills to pay, you worry about keeping your job, and you just worry about everything.

When you live debt free – you have more peace of mind. There are still other trials and tribulations in life, but why add to your burden.

Living debt free also give you the ability to save for the future (cars, college, weddings, retirement) and plan for unexpected events (broken appliances, tree falling on house, home repairs, health issues, serious car breakdown etc.).

The peace of mind from being debt free also gives you clarity of thought and the ability to be more generous.

A Tale of Two People

My Bride was a spender and I am a saver! Do you see some potential for conflict?

When we first got married, I had zero debt and my Bride had quite a bit of debt. She had a car payment and she owned a house.   Her car payment was $400 per month (at 23% interest) and her house payment was $1,200 per month (at 14% interest).   Her take home pay was not much more than these combined payments. She was living on the very edge of financial disaster.   When you include, food, clothing, fuel and utilities, she was living beyond her means.   Needless to say, this was not a sustainable way to live.

I had no debt whatsoever and I was freaking out when I found out she was living this way.

After we were married, the first thing we did was pay her car off ($8,000). The second thing we did was refinance the mortgage to 9% (which was a fantastic rate back in the day).   From that day until this, we have been aligned on our hatred of debt and the problems it brings.
The only debt that we have in our lives is the mortgage on our house. We have a 15 year loan and we cannot wait to pay it off!

How do we avoid debt?

We don't spend more than we make! We pay cash! When the cash is gone, the spending stops. You probably say – that is too simple. Yep!

Simple works. It does not take a rocket scientist (no offense to rocket scientist) to figure this out.

You might say, what about cars?? You cannot possibly pay cash for cars, they are too expensive. Well, I know a guy! He calls himself the "Camry Man" and we buy good used cars for about $4,000 to $5,000 in cash. They are usually about 10 years old and will require a little more maintenance and "love".

However, even if I spend $1,000 per year fixing them (which has never happened) this would only equate to $83 per month. The key is having an emergency fund available (which we do) to pay for any repair. Then you don't sweat driving an older car. Is there some risk involved? Sure there is. I am no mechanic, but I do all the key basic maintenance to keep the cars running smoothly. Also, we invest in AAA program that will give us peace of mind if we need roadside service or towing.

You see, we would rather have the risk of breakdown (which rarely happens anyway) than have the debt hanging over our heads.

According to Experian, the average new car payment is $493 per month and the average used car payment is $359 per month. That means most people are paying between $4,300 and $5,900 per year on car payments. If you spent $2,000 per year on repairs, you would still be ahead of the game!

My current car is a 2000 Toyota Camry with 260,000 miles on it. I commute almost 90 miles per day. I have had this car for 6 years and I bought it when it had 150,000 miles on it. My Bride drives a 2005 Toyota Highlander and we got it with 170,000 miles on it. We have yet to have a major breakdown with either car.

We are very careful when we buy our used cars. We research them, test them and do not buy unless we can pay cash and all of the indicators point to a reliable vehicle (one owner, no wrecks, maintenance checks etc.)

What about college? We saved money and are paying cash!   Our kids also have jobs and pay for all of their own expenses (car, gas, insurance, cell phone, cloths, eating out etc).   The best gift we can give our children is to have them graduate with no debt!   Is it tough? Yes. Do we make sacrifices? Yes. My oldest daughter just graduated this year from the University of Georgia (go Bulldogs) with a double major and has ZERO student loan debt.   It took a little longer, but was worth the wait.

I pack a lunch to work every day! I don't eat out (except on a date with my Bride).   Debbie shops at the thrift store for most of our cloths (you would be amazed at the bargains you can get).

Debt owns most people! It dictates their life and what they can and cannot do.   They do not control the money the money controls them.

We hate debt with a passion! You need to hate it as well! Take control of your finances and eliminate one of the key sources of conflict in a marriage.

Avoid credit cards at all costs!   They are an avenue of easy money and very few people can control them. Some will say – I use them for points or rewards or cash back and I pay the bill in full each month.

Congratulations, you are a very small percent of the population.   You still have the issue of controlling your spending, because unless you keep close watch over every receipt, you cannot know what you have spent each month until the bill comes. With the cash method, you can never over spend. However, the vast majority of people make credit card payment each month and it is killing them. Cut up your cards and start spending cash instead.

My Aunt recently passed away and we had to close out her estate.   We were shocked to find out that her credit card debt was equal to ½ of her annual salary.   It is a real mess we have to clean up now.

My Bride and I have been walking the debt-free journey for a while now and we see and feel the benefits each and every day.   While we have to make short-term sacrifices, we have begun to reap the long-term benefits.

A great definition of discipline = delayed gratification!   When you have financial discipline, you may not have all of your immediate "wants" but you will have the long-term gratification of meeting your goals.

Set Financial Goals and a Budget Together

Let me start by saying that I am a huge fan of Dave Ramsey, so if you know the principles that he shares and what he believes, then a lot of this material will seem very familiar. If you do not know Dave Ramsey, I would highly encourage you to listen to his radio show and read his books. It is very easy and practical advice. I was actually doing many of the principles that he taught long before I become a listener to his show.

Setting goals may be new for some of you and for others it is old hat. Many of you set goals in your life for different things but not how you deal with your money. Here are some common goals people set:

- Lose 10 lbs. in 2 weeks
- Learn a new language
- Run a marathon

You see we all have goals, but many times they are only mental or perhaps verbal, but seldom are they actually written down. I am going to encourage you to use the SMART method for setting your financial goals.

S = specific
M = measurable
A= actionable
R= realistic
T = time bound (and or time limit)

In addition to setting SMART goals you are much more likely to complete your goals if they are written down.

With that said, let's talk about the money!

Since you don't want money to be a point of contention or problem in your marriage, setting these goals together is key. You must be completely aligned on the goals and hold each other accountable to keeping them.

When Debbie and I got married, we brought into the marriage two very different philosophies on money. She was a spender and I was a saver. She had grown up in a very safe and comfortable middle class life style and I had grown up rather poor and in distress at times.

We knew we would need to reconcile our differences or else they could tear us apart.

We sat down and talked about what was important in our lives and where we wanted to invest our money. This did not happen overnight and it has evolved throughout our marriage, but the key is that we are aligned and in agreement on these overarching goals.

Here are the big buckets that we use to classify the money (a Dave Ramsey principle is to know where each and every dollar is going.) I am not going to get that specific; I want you to understand the concept of having the goals and gaining alignment with your spouse.

- Monthly Bills – utilities etc.
- Charity/Gifts
- Retirement
- School & College
- Emergency Funds
- Vacation
- Specific savings – cars, appliances, other big purchases

You see, if you don't have a goal and plans, then money will just slip through your hands and this will ultimately lead to conflict (because bills will not get paid, dreams will not be made, and stress will enter your life)

I want to juxtapose examples of non-smart goals and SMART goals. We will assume this family makes $60,000 per year and has one son who is 8 years old

Non-smart goal

We want to save money for our son's college expenses.

While this may sound good, it is too vague, not measurable, and not time-bound.

SMART goal

We want to save $20,000 over the next 10 years for our son's college expenses. We will save $167 each month starting next month and invest the money in a 529 savings plan.

This goal meets all of the criteria to be a SMART goal

Specific – Money for son's college into a 529 plan
Measurable - $20,000 (or $167 each month)
Actionable – start next month
Reasonable – on a monthly basis this is about 3.3% of their income.
Time-bound – each month for the next 10 years

But does something like this really work? It sure does.

I have four children and we have put two of them through college without debt and for my youngest two children we have very systematic savings (twice per month) and we started that 529 savings plan the same month they were born.

My two youngest are now in their teens and we a substantial amount of money saved and should not have any need to borrow money for college. Did we have to a sacrifice? Yes of course we had to sacrifice (that is why we drive old cars, take our lunch to work, shop at the thrift store and don't eat out much).

For those more immediate needs, you need to have a family "operating" budget. These are the day to day, week to week recurring items in your life. Each of these should have a specific amount allocated and then you never spend more than that amount. If you put aside $400 per month for groceries, then when the $400 is spent for that month you stop buying groceries. It will force you to consider how each dollar is spent.

- Household (the day to day operating expenses – utilities, food, cleaning supplies, repairs etc.)
- Auto – (insurance, gas, taxes and maintenance)
- Entertainment
- Tithe
- Mortgage

Setting up a budget is somewhat easier than the goals, because you have the past history of what you have spent. You know about how much you spend on utilities each month.

When you have this budget figured out, then you know how much is left over for the bigger goals in your life.

Again, I encourage you to visit www.daveramsey.com and look under the tools folder. You will find more than enough resources to help you.

Avoid debt – Especially Credit Card Debt

Here is a more detailed list of what it means for us to be Economically Sound:

- Don't spend more than we make (live within our budget)
- Save more for:
    - College
    - Weddings
    - Emergencies
    - Repairs
    - Cars
    - Retirement
    - Vacation
    - Holidays
    - Birthdays and special occasions
- Spend Less
    - Look for bargains
    - Shop at thrift stores
    - Pack your lunch
    - Eat out less
    - Pay cash for cars
    - Negotiate where possible
- No debt
    - No Credit Card
    - No second mortgage
    - No borrowing from friends or family
    - We do not co-sign for anything or anybody – ever!
- Being generous
    - Church
    - Missions
    - Family
    - Friends
- Rent instead of owning depreciating assets (things like boats, jet skis, ATV.s RV's, motorcycles)

Ultimately, the choice is yours! How will you manage your treasures?

Choices

What Choices do we face when considering our economic future?

- To save
- To spend
- To give
- To invest

First, let us consider the ample warning from the Bible in regards to money. Here are two key warnings to consider.

- Don't fall in love with money
- You can only serve one master

1 Timothy 6:10

For the love of money is a root of all sorts of evil, and some by longing for it have wandered away from the faith and pierced themselves with many grief's.

Hebrews 13:5

Make sure that your character is free from the love of money, being content with what you have; for He Himself has said, "I will never desert you, nor will I ever forsake you,"

Matthew 16:26

For what will it profit a man if he gains the whole world and forfeits his soul? Or what will a man give in exchange for his soul?

Matthew 6:24

No one can serve two masters; for either he will hate the one and love the other, or he will be devoted to one and despise the other. You cannot serve God and wealth.

These verses are a clear warning to us in regards to money. Look at some of the key words and phrases and you know that you will have to be diligent to ward off the dangers of the love of money. The good news is there are two things you can do to keep from falling into this trap.

The first thing you can do is learn to be content. Contentment means you are forgoing your current desires and you are pleased with what you have. Later in the book you will find a whole section about contentment and being content and the example with have from the Apostle Paul. If you want to skip ahead, start by reading and mediating on the book of Philippian's. Paul talks extensively about joy and contentment (which is important, because he was writing this book while in chains in prison).

The second thing you can do is choose to serve God. When you are serving and following God, your wants and desires will change. Especially if you really start to see the world through the same lens which God views the world (a lost and dying generation in need of a Savior and salvation)

Debt and Borrowing

- Don't borrow money
- But if you do, then make sure to pay it back!
- Do not guarantee debt for others!

Proverbs 22:7

The rich rules over the poor,
And the borrower becomes the lender's slave.

Psalm 37:21

The wicked borrows and does not pay back,
But the righteous is gracious and gives.

Proverbs 22:26

Do not be among those who give pledges,
Among those who become guarantors for debts.

Proverbs 11:15

He who is guarantor for a stranger will surely suffer for it,
But he who hates being a guarantor is secure.

Ecclesiastes 5:5

It is better that you should not vow than that you should vow and not pay.

Save & Be Prepared

It is important to be prepared and save for the rainy day (or for the season when there is no rain). Consider Joseph in Egypt as he interprets Pharaohs dream and tells him there will be 7 years of plenty and 7 years of famine.

Pharaoh is so impressed with Joseph, he asks him what can be done to save the nation from this disaster, and Joseph tells him to store up 20% of the grain during the years of plenty. It is a sound plan and does indeed not only save the nation of Egypt, but also Joseph's family.

Genesis 41:33-36

Now let Pharaoh look for a man discerning and wise, and set him over the land of Egypt. Let Pharaoh take action to appoint overseers in charge of the land, and let him exact a fifth of the produce of the land of Egypt in the seven years of abundance. Then let them gather all the food of these good years that are coming, and store up the grain for food in the cities under Pharaoh's authority, and let them guard it. Let the food become as a reserve for the land for the seven years of famine which will occur in the land of Egypt, so that the land will not perish during the famine."

Proverbs tell us to consider the ants. They are small creatures indeed and yet they gather their food in the summer and fall so there is plenty when the harsh days of winter are upon them.

Proverbs 30:24-25

Four things are small on the earth,
But they are exceedingly wise:
The ants are not a strong people,
But they prepare their food in the summer;

Proverbs also tells us that a wise and prudent man can see danger coming from afar and will prepare for that as well. It is not "if" you will have storms, trials or tribulations in your life, it is "when". Some you can see coming (like a Hurricane) and others are a complete surprise. It is best to have that rainy day fund set aside so you can weather the storm.

<u>Rainy day savings</u> – I actually have three different rainy day savings.

a. **Spring shower savings** – this is for the little stuff that comes up and bites you in the rear end. They are generally expenses under $10,000 and can be handled out of this fund. We usually tap into this fund several times per year and then replenish it again. This money is kept in a standard saving account at my primary bank and is very easy to access. Examples of things we use this for:
   i. Transmission going out on a car
   ii. Broken water heater
   iii. Air conditioner replacement

b. **Summer Thunderstorm saving** – this is for more catastrophic things that could happen. My deductible for home owners insurance is $10,000 – so this fund would be tapped into help with something major happening to the house or for some type of serious medical problem. We keep this money in a separate Credit Union that is very difficult to get to. The Credit Union is farther from our house and we do not have any debit cards or ATM cards to access the money, nor can we access the money on-line in any way. We have to physically go into the local branch to get the money. It is a very intentional act on our part to keep this money at a distance and difficult to reach. If it were easy to access, we might be tempted to use if for a non-emergency.

c. **Hurricane saving** – this is about six months' worth of expenses that is held in a separate investment house and it is NEVER to be touched except in the loss of employment. This money is VERY hard to get to, and it is a real pain to access! We praise God that we have never had to tap into this money yet!

Proverbs 21:5

The plans of the diligent lead surely to advantage,
But everyone who is hasty comes surely to poverty.

Proverbs 21:20

There is precious treasure and oil in the dwelling of the wise,
But a foolish man swallows it up.

Proverbs 13:22

A good man leaves an inheritance to his children's children,
And the wealth of the sinner is stored up for the righteous.

Proverbs 27:12
A prudent man sees evil and hides himself,
The naive proceed and pay the penalty.

Additional, we are told to consider our flocks and the condition or our herd.

Proverbs 27:23

Know well the condition of your flocks,
And pay attention to your herds;

While few of us today have flocks or herds, what would be analogous today would be our business, household, checking and savings accounts and all of the equipment and resources God has put at our disposal. We are called to be good stewards of these possessions so that we can take care of our family, but also so we can be a blessing to others and help to meet their needs as well. The resources God has placed in our hands are not just for us and our own wants, needs and desires. They are to be used to bless others and help meet their needs as well.

Will you choose today to be a saver? Will you choose to be prepared? Will you choose to forgo pleasures today and exercise financial discipline by saving?

<u>Giving</u>

"You are never more like Jesus than when you are giving."
Johnny Hunt

I know of only one way to deal with my own selfishness and greed and that is to be a generous giver.   It is the only antidote that works 100% of the time.   You get to bless others and in return you get blessed.   Giving creates and sustains a beautiful cycle of generosity – not only material wealth, but encouragement as well.

God loves a cheerful giver and expects us to give back a portion, which He has already given us.   Think of it this way.   God has given you ALL that you have, so it all originally belongs to God to start with.   When you give back to God, you are only giving back what had belonged to God to begin with.

Consider the generosity of King David when it was time to build the temple for God.   David would not be allowed to build the temple (his son Solomon would build the temple).   However, David could raise the funds and make it possible to build the temple.

How much did David give?   He gave 3,000 talents of the finest gold and 7,000 talents of silver.

Now this may not sound like much because we are not familiar with these finance measures.   A talent = 75lbs.   So David gave 225,000lbs of gold 525,000lbs of silver.   How much does that equate to today?   Well, gold is about $1,250 per ounce and silver is $17.00 per ounce, so that is about $4.5 billion dollars that David gave to build the temple.   This is generosity by any stretch of the imagination. Of course, this does not include the wood, jewels, iron, bronze, alabaster and other materials that he also provided.

David was a cheerful and thoughtful giver.   He was a man after God's own heart and he wanted to honor God and create a temple worthy of God.

Will you choose to be a giver?   Will you be intentional about your giving and choose to be a cheerful giver?

2 Corinthians 9:6-7

Now this I say, he who sows sparingly will also reap sparingly, and he who sows bountifully will also reap bountifully. Each one must do just as he has purposed in his heart, not grudgingly or under compulsion, for <u>God loves a cheerful giver.</u>

1 Chronicles 29:3-5

Moreover, in my delight in the house of my God, the treasure I have of gold and silver, I give to the house of my God, over and above all that I have already provided for the holy temple, namely, 3,000 talents of gold, of the gold of Ophir, and 7,000 talents of refined silver, to overlay the walls of the buildings; of gold for the things of gold and of silver for the things of silver, that is, for all the work done by the craftsmen. Who then is willing to consecrate himself this day to the Lord?"

Proverbs 3:9-10

*Honor the Lord from your wealth
And from the first of all your produce;
So your barns will be filled with plenty
And your vats will overflow with new wine.*

Malachi 3:10

Bring the whole tithe into the storehouse, so that there may be food in My house, and test Me now in this," says the Lord of hosts, "if I will not open for you the windows of heaven and pour out for you a blessing until it overflows.

Proverbs 11:24

*There is one who scatters, and yet increases all the more,
And there is one who withholds what is justly due, and yet it results only in want.*

Tough Questions:

- Are you a good steward of your financial resources?

- Would your family and friends say you are a good steward?

- Does your bank statement say you are a good steward?

- Are you saving more?

- Are you spending less?

- Can you be more generous?

- Do you have a budget and follow it?

- Do you serve money and possessions or do they serve you?

- What is the toughest area of your finances to control?

- If you are married, are you aligned on spending, saving, giving, generosity and goals? If not, why not?

Mentally Positive

"Your attitude, not your aptitude, will determine your altitude."
Zig Ziglar

I love this quote above by Zig Ziglar. It is used by people all the time and it is a simple universal truth. Attitude is everything! Your attitude will determine how you view the world and all of the circumstances that come your way.

Would you rather hang out with someone who is positive most of the time or negative most of the time? My guess is you would rather hang out with the person who has the positive attitude most of the time.

I had a friend of mine at work who was absolutely brilliant! He knew this company inside out and upside down. He was a go to person for information and insight. Unfortunately, he was also one of the most negative people you could ever know.

With him, everything was a conspiracy (or so it seemed), the world was out to get him and everybody had a grudge against him. At least once per week I had to talk him off the ledge.

All of his brilliance did not matter at the end of the day, because his negative attitude drove people away. He was never able to advance his career or really influence the organization, because people could not get past his negative attitude.

He eventually retired a few years ago and has tried to calm down and settle in, but even to this day, he is not someone you want to spend a lot of time with.

Attitude has consequences both short and long term, in the home and in the work place, as well as at church and in the community and neighborhood.

One of my early jobs was horrible! I had a horrible boss, horrible accounts and a horrible team. In reality, I had a horrible attitude. This was reflected in my sales results – very poor and my relationship with my boss and team – strained.

It took some extreme talks with my Bride, some soul searching, prayer and repentance to turn things around.

Suddenly, I had a great boss, great accounts and a great team! What changed? Nothing....except my attitude. These were the same people, accounts and team, but I had changed (for the better). I CHOOSE to have a positive attitude and it really did change everything. There were still challenges and obstacles to overcome, but nothing was insurmountable.

Are you a glass half full or glass half empty type of person? Be honest now. If I am totally honest, I have to tell you that I have been a glass half-full person most of my life. I like to use excuses such as:

- "I am a realist"
- "Most people are not trustworthy"
- "The world does not work that way"

In the end, these are all excuses, because a having positive attitude is 100% my choice. It is 100% your choice as well!

Questions:

- Should we have a positive attitude?

- Are there benefits to having a positive attitude?

- Is attitude a choice?

An Injured Leg

I love to run! I have been a serious runner for over 40 years and running is part of my DNA. I love the solitude, the challenge, the sweat and work. I love to push myself and feel my body working. When friends from college or high school see me, they always ask if I am still running, because running has been such a defining part of my life.

As I entered my 50's, running was not as easy (I was slower and that is always humbling) and the aches and pains seemed to last longer. In spite of these troubles, I still ventured out every day, rain or shine, cold or hot.

I wanted to feel the road beneath my feet. Nothing was better than finding a beautiful nature trail and heading off into the woods for a long run.

About 4 months ago, I was on a run and I felt a "catch" in my Achilles heel on my right leg. I have been incredibly blessed over the years to have few injuries and I was not worried about this. It did not hobble me or stop me from running, but it was just a little sore.

I continued to run and exercise and then about a week later, I was stopped dead in my tracks after about 11 minutes of running. My right leg was in too much pain. I chalked it up to overuse and decided I needed to rest for a few days.

I followed the prescribed R.I.C.E. procedure (rest, ice, compression, elevation) for three days and figured I was cured. I was able to walk without pain and it seemed fine.

I took off for my run and after about 10 minutes the pain was so intense I had to stop. To say I was angry and frustrated would be an understatement. However, this was short lived and I figured I had not given it enough time to heal. I then took a week off (something I had not done in decades) and tried again. Same result!!

I was at a cross roads. There was a flood of emotions washing over me as I realized I would not be able to run for a long time. What was I to do with myself? Running had always defined me and was just part of who I was. I felt like part of me was missing.

I knew I had a choice to make and the choice was clear.   I had been focusing my energy and attention on being intentional in all aspects of my life and I was also learning about the significance of my attitude and choices.

I told you earlier in the chapter that I had been a glass half empty kind of person and I could have easily let this injury take me down the road of depression, confusion and anger.

Instead I choose a different path.   I took the path less traveled.

I choose to praise God for the injury and the opportunities it would afford me to exercise in a different way.

I choose to be thankful for the injury and thankful that I could still walk and get around. I decided to be thankful for all the things I could do, instead of complaining about the one thing I could not do.

Therefore, for the past 4 months I have discovered the joys of weight lifting, calisthenics, core body work and other exercises.

I had never been serious about core body work or calisthenics. It seemed too hard and time consuming to do right.   What I found was that it was hard and took time to do it right!   It was going to be hard work.

I started out that first week and my routine was simple.   I would try to do five pushups (three times) and I would try to do five crunches (three times).   It was painful! I could barely do five pushups and the crunches were painful (especially the next day).

However I choose to be thankful for what I could do and not be angry about what I could not do.

Week by week I would add to my routine.   The next week I did six pushups and 6 crunches (three sets of each).   I did this 6 days a week. I continued this week by week until I worked up to ten of each exercise and five sets of each one. This took me 6 weeks to get to that point.

Once I was there, I could see the positive change in my body and now I really began to push myself.   It has been over four months now and I can do 300-400 pushups and 1,000 different core exercises at one time.   (I moved beyond crunches to include 15 different core exercises).   I also added some weight lifting and work with kettle bells.

I may never be able to run again.   I will try again soon, but I will praise God for what I can do and not worry about what I cannot do.   It is my choice and I choose to be thankful.   I decided that being physically fit was more than just running and I am glad the injury has helped me to develop a more whole body workout approach.

When I ran, it was a solitary thing I did. However, the other benefits of this injury are that I have been walking with my Beautiful Bride as she has been influenced by my routine and has started down this same path herself.   I have also been lifting weights with my son and spending some additional time with him.

Will I run again?   I hope so?   However, God has given me a real contentment and peace that I did not think was possible without running.

I choose to be thankful! Attitude is everything.   I will continue to focus on what is possible and reject the negative thoughts.

Glass Half Empty

I just gave you an example of where I did a good job of handling my attitude, now let me share a quick story of how my glass half empty attitude gets me in trouble with my Bride.

As I told you in the first chapter my son Jonathan is playing football for the first time. It has been a very frustrating experience for me as a father to watch the team go 0-6 and score only three touchdowns!   We have a young team that is small and somewhat slow (compared to the competition), we also have great coaches, but fierce competition.   Every game we have played this season has ended with the "mercy rule" in effect whereby they let the game clock run out in the 4th quarter without stopping.

I tend to watch the game and point out the "flaws" and offer what I view as realistic commentary about the current situation. While I may feel justified in my "analysis", my Bride chooses to see every situation through a different lens. In addition, she does not appreciate my analysis or commentary. More than once she has given me the "school teacher" look (yes all you men know what that look means).

We are watching the same game and we see the same plays and yet we approach how we choose to view the game differently. Let me give you an example.

It was late in the game and we had not moved the ball effectively all game long. Finally the boys broke out and got a first down! Now we were behind 38-0, but you would have thought we had just scored a touchdown.

On the next play, we went for a pass and it was almost intercepted – or at least that is how I saw the play. I started to complain to my Bride that we should not be passing the ball and giving the other team the chance to intercept late in the game. She looked at me in all sincerity said " our player almost caught that ball, it was very close". We both saw the exact same play (it was literally right in front of us) and we had two different attitudes about the outcome. It was very revealing to me.

I continued to argue the "logical" view of what I saw and my Bride was steadfast that our team almost caught the ball and it would have been great.

Clearly I have a long way to go when it comes to having a positive attitude! I am so glad I have my beautiful Bride by my side as an encourager and accountability partner, but more importantly, as a living example of someone who chooses to have a glass half full attitude. She has been and continues to be a shining light in the darkness for me and our family.

Having a positive attitude will have to be a CHOICE for me! It does not come naturally and I know I will have to be on my guard when negativity starts to seep into my mind and fill me with negative thoughts and attitudes..

Let's look at a couple of characters from the Bible and see what kind of attitude they had when they were faced with difficult situations and choices.

Shadrach, Meshach, and Abednego

Talk about trouble! Your country is invaded (most likely you have had friends and relatives killed in the battles) and you get carted off to a foreign land as bounty for the king.

Not only are you stripped of you nationality, you are even given a new name and forced to learn the language and customs of your captors.

This is the situation we find Hananiah, Mishael and Azariah – now these names are not nearly as familiar as the names there were given by their captors - Shadrach, Meshach, and Abednego (or if you are a fan of Veggie Tales – Rack, Shack and Benny).

These three young men find themselves in a foreign land and yet they choose to continue to worship their God and retain their Jewish heritage.   They are captives of the Babylonians and it is King Nebuchadnezzar who had ordered them brought out of their land into Babylon.

The good news is that the king was really impressed with these guys and wants them to work directly for him in his personal service. The bad news is that they are captives in a foreign land, so it's not like they had a lot of choice in the matter.

The king decides to make a golden statue and commands all of the people to fall down and worship this golden idol. Oh, and by the way there is one small consideration if you don't bow down and worship – you immediately get thrown in a huge oven and get burned to death.

Let's pick up the story from there in Daniel Chapter 3

Daniel 3:6

But whoever does not fall down and worship shall immediately be cast into the midst of a furnace of blazing fire."

So it is pretty unequivocal what the king wants. He wants everybody to worship this idol. It will also be pretty easy to see who is not worshiping the idol, because they will be the ones standing while everybody else is falling to their faces (in fear of death instead of worship to this idol).

Shadrach, Meshach, and Abednego refuse to worship this idol and are called out by others in the king's court. The king is considerably angry and brings them in for questioning. He is going to give them one last chance before he lowers the "boom".

Daniel 3:15

"Now if you are ready, at the moment you hear the sound of the horn, flute, lyre, trigon, psaltery and bagpipe and all kinds of music, to fall down and worship the image that I have made, very well. But if you do not worship, you will immediately be cast into the midst of a furnace of blazing fire; and what god is there who can deliver you out of my hands?"

I love their reply to the king. It brings with it - confidence, hope, adoration and worship all wrapped together

Daniel 3:16-18

Shadrach, Meshach and Abednego replied to the king, "O Nebuchadnezzar, we do not need to give you an answer concerning this matter. If it be so, our God whom we serve is able to deliver us from the furnace of blazing fire; and He will deliver us out of your hand, O king. But even if He does not, let it be known to you, O king, that we are not going to serve your gods or worship the golden image that you have set up."

What happens to them? They are thrown in the fiery furnace! It is heated to a temperature that was so hot and the king was so mad that the soldiers who cast them into the furnace perished because they acted so quickly.

In the end, God did deliver them from the fiery furnace and the King declared that nobody would say anything offensive about the God of Shadrach, Meshach, and Abednego.

Their attitude and actions in this situation are cause for celebration! They have a clear choice set before them and they choose to do the right thing, in spite of the consequences.

<u>Action</u> – speak up and stand up against evil

<u>Attitude</u> – we do not care what happens to us because we have faith in our God no matter what happens

Very few of us will ever face a test as dreadful as this one.   What we learn from this lesson is that no matter what our circumstances, we do have a choice of our attitude and actions.

Finally, I would advocate that they were prepared for this situation because of their own personal relationship with God, their study of His Word and the praise and worship of they were offering Him.

They knew from their teachings as Jews that there was only ONE GOD and they would only serve, honor and worship Him.   They knew how God had delivered the Jewish nation from captivity in Egypt and they would have known of His other miracles and deliverance.

It is important to note that their attitude and actions were born out of a faith in the ONE TRUE GOD! Without faith it is impossible to please God.

They made the choice to have a positive attitude in the face of a difficult decision..   Their choice was born out of a life of study, prayer, fellowship and worship. We have that same opportunity to prepare ourselves for the day of difficult decisions and challenges.   It is not "if" we will face trials and tribulations, but "when".

Will you make the choice to be prepared?

Paul and the Philippians

Paul is writing to the Philippians in Macedonia while he himself is in chains! He tells them to "Rejoice in the Lord always; again I will say rejoice!" Paul was the living embodiment of the right attitude. He is in Rome, in prison, in chains. Yet he pens this beautiful letter of Philippians and it is filled with joy and encouragement.

Paul uses the word JOY or REJOICING fifteen times in the book of Philippians

How is this possible? It is possible because he chooses to have a positive attitude. He does not let his circumstances dictate his actions. He will continue to exhibit the fruits of the spirit until the day he dies. He has also learned to be content in each and every circumstance of life.

I believe the verses below are an excellent example of Paul encouraging the believer to have the right attitude (and he knew that good actions would follow the proper attitude).

Choices for being Mentally Positive:

Here are two key choices to consider as you look towards having a positive attitude.

- Choose to focus on the good things!
- Choose to be content!

Philippians 4:8-9 – Focusing on the good things

Finally, brethren, whatever is true, whatever is honorable, whatever is right, whatever is pure, whatever is lovely, whatever is of good repute, if there is any excellence and if anything worthy of praise, dwell on these things. The things you have learned and received and heard and seen in me, practice these things, and the God of peace will be with you.

In this these verses you can clearly see the call to focus our mind, energy and attention on whatever is:

- True
- Honorable
- Right
- Pure
- Lovely
- Of good Rrepute
- Of Excellence
- Worthy of praise

We are called to dwell on these things. This means to think, contemplate, mediate, and take into our hearts. If we spend our time on these things, it does not give us time to focus on the negatives of life (which is too easy to do).

Contentment

Philippians 4:12-13

I know how to get along with humble means, and I also know how to live in prosperity; in any and every circumstance I have learned the secret of being filled and going hungry, both of having abundance and suffering need. I can do all things through Him who strengthens me.

Philippians 4:11

Not that I speak from want, for I have learned to be content in whatever circumstances I am

Contentment is something we choose. Nobody can thrust contentment upon us, like a man thrusting a sword into his enemy. Contentment is something we strive for and seek to achieve in our minds, for that is where the battle ground for contentment if fought. Do I have enough? Can I have more? I want more! I need more! I desire more?

When is enough, enough? Only by trusting God to be your complete provider and protector will you ever have "enough". It is when you realize that God is enough to satisfy all of your wants, needs and desires.

Paul says it well:

Philippians 4:13

I can do all things through Him (Christ) *who strengthens me.*

Choose today to be content with what you have, where you are!   To be clear, contentment does not mean resignation.   We are not resigned to our fate or circumstances.   Contentment is about attitude and the positive actions that will follow that positive attitude.

Choose today to be content!

Why we should have Positive Attitude?

Philippians 2:14-16

Do all things without grumbling or disputing; so that you will prove yourselves to be blameless and innocent, children of God above reproach in the midst of a crooked and perverse generation, among whom you appear as lights in the world, holding fast the word of life, so that in the day of Christ I will have reason to glory because I did not run in vain nor toil in vain.

We need to have a positive attitude because others are watching us. Our family, friends, co-workers, neighbors and others have their eye upon us. Especially if they know we claim to be Christians and followers of Christ.

We are called to be a light unto the world and provide a positive testimony for the hope we have within us.

Who would want to have the same relationship with Christ that we have, if all they see is a negative attitude and lack of contentment.   That will not draw anyone to Christ.

However, if they see us with a positive attitude and contentment in the midst of a dark and dying world, then we become the light that shows the way to Christ and salvation.

Paul kept it simple and so will I. I have found a little word that can help transform your thinking and attitude. I have found this very useful in both my personal life (especially with my children) as well as the work place and at church.

It is the word – **"YET"**

This wonderful little word can turn negative statements into positive statements.

Examples:

- This product line is not profitable.
- I don't know how to play football.
- The Sunday School classes are not engaged.
- I have not finished that book.
- We will never figure this out.

Turn these statements around and add the word yet.

- This product line is not profitable, yet.
- I don't know how to play football, yet.
- The Sunday School classes are not engaged, yet.
- I have not finished that book, yet.
- We have not figured this out yet.

Adding the word "yet" leads to a positive discussion and changes the discourse. It is a small word, with a powerful impact. But it only works if you choose to use it. It will take some practice and it might seem contrived at first, but give it time and it will soon become second nature.

Some of you may say you cannot do it, and I say you have just not done it YET!

Benefits of a Positive Attitude

Are there benefits to having a positive attitude? There sure are!
According to our good friends at the Mayo Clinic, extensive research has
shown there are some real tangible benefits to having a positive attitude.

- Increased life span
- Lower rates of depression
- Lower levels of distress
- Greater resistance to the common cold
- Better psychological and physical well-being
- Better cardiovascular health and reduced risk of death from cardiovascular disease
- Better coping skills during hardships and times of stress

Isn't it interesting that we have research that show you can extend you
lifespan by having a regular exercise routine, and now here is some
additional research that says you can increase your lifespan by having a
positive attitude. If you combine the two of these, there is no telling how
long you will live.

Of course nobody knows how many days they have to walk this earth, but
wouldn't you rather walk this path with a positive attitude and outlook on
life. It appears to me the grass will seem greener, the sky a more brilliant
blue, people more pleasant and life is worth living to its fullest.

Perhaps that is just me being glass half full!

Is Attitude a Choice?

What do you think? Is your attitude your choice? Do you have 100%
control of your attitude (and your actions)? Can someone force you to
have a good or bad attitude?

Your attitude is 100% your choice. You may not get to choose the
circumstances, but you always get to choose your response and your
attitude.

I always find it interesting when I write about a subject or topic, inevitably, I will be faced with a situation where I have to live up to my own writing and beliefs. Believe me when I say it is much easier to write about this stuff than actually live it out in this messy world we live in.

When my son and I were camping deep in the woods, I had a flat tire. Now being the Uber Prepared person who has had flat tires in the woods before, I thought I had it handled. I had a small air compressor for refilling the tire (it was some type of slow leak and not a blowout).

In this way, I could just refill the tire with air and then just stay in the woods camping and just keep refilling the tire as needed. Usually with a slow leak I could few hours before it went flat again. I was over an hour to get to town and the drive would be on old gravel roads, so I would rather stay in the woods if possible an not disturb the trip.

Then Murphy's Law kicked into high gear.

The air compressor worked for about five minutes and then it began to smoke and sputter and then it just quit. It was brand new! I literally took it out of the box to use it on this tire. I had used this same type of compressor many times before on my other cars and have had great success.

Good thing I had that can of "Fix-A-Flat" as well. I had only used Fix-A-Flat once before and it had performed as needed. However, it was a measure last resort, because if I used it I knew I would only have a short period of time to get back into town and get the tire fixed and or pick up a new air compressor and new cans of Fix-A-Flat. We were headed to town.

Where we got to town the only place open that could fix my tire was Wal-Mart. They told me with delight that they indeed could fix my tire and the wait would only be 3 ½ hours. It was raining, cold and there was nothing in the vicinity to keep us occupied for 3 ½ hours. I reluctantly gave up my keys and was resigned to my fate, and then it struck we that I had been looking to finish well and have a good attitude.

My youngest son Jonathan was with me, so I told him about our dilemma and our choice to have a good attitude. I told him we could choose to make the most of this time and make a memory or we could be miserable. Either way, 3 ½ hours would pass and we would either be joyful or miserable. It was our choice.

We chose joy!   We took stock of what to be thankful for – we were dressed for cold rainy weather, we were in a warm and safe environment and it was Saturday – so I was not working and he was not doing school. There was a lot to be thankful for this day.

As we took stock, we realized it was 2:30 pm and we had missed lunch. Our stomachs cried out for food and we were blessed to have money and several choices within walking distanced (in the rain).

I let Jonathan choose and we could see off in the distance a Chick-Fil-A and we both loved their foods, so we hoofed it on over there and found good food and drink as well as free Wi-Fi.

We had completely forgotten that Georgia was playing Florida at 3:30 and the game would be on CBS, therefore we could stream it live on my phone. We did not think we would see the game because there is no cell service where we were camping.

We then spent the next few hours at Chick-Fil-A, filling ourselves with chicken, fries and ice cream and watching a great game. It was a fun and memorable experience and the time flew by. Before we knew it that tire was fixed and we were on our way.   We listed to the end of the game on the radio as we headed back into the woods.

We had a choice to make in a circumstance that we did not choose. We intentionally chose to be joyful!   Yes we chose that joyful/positive attitude. It was not our first instinct, but it was our choice.

I can tell you that before I intentionally started on this journey to be intentional and finish well, that 3 ½ hours would have been miserable for me and everyone around me (I would have ensured everybody was equally miserable – misery loves company).

Do not take lightly the power you have within you to choose! It is almost a super power that can reenergize your life.   Look out Superman!

You may be thinking to yourself, nobody understands what I have been through or what I am going through.

That may be true, but there are very few (if any) unique circumstances in life and bad things happen to good people all the time.   Let me leave you with this story.

During World War II, there was a priest who was imprisoned in one of the many Nazi death camps.   He had done nothing wrong, except to speak up against the evil he had seen all around him.

One day a prisoner from his building escaped. The punishment for an escaped prisoner was to take 10 innocent people from that same building and lock them in the basement without food or water until they died. It was a horrible way to perish.

As the guards picked 10 people at random, one man who was chosen begged for his life and asked to be spared.   Since mercy and compassion were not a known by the guards, he was beaten and ridiculed.

However, this priest stepped forward and asked to take the place of this man.   The guards did not care who lived or died, they just needed 10 bodies. So they allowed the priest to take this man's place.

The 10 prisoners were thrown into the basement and everybody knew what was coming, because this had happened many times in the past. They knew there would be screaming and wailing and unbelievable noises.

As the days passed, not a sound was heard except for some soft singing and words of prayer and praise. The priest was leading the men through the valley of the shadow of death and as a good shepherd he chose to have a good attitude and to recognize he could help these men in these last desperate days. He chose to go, he chose to lead, he chose to pray, he chose to sing, and he chose to praise.

Everyone was amazed and when 10 days had passed most of the men were dead, but the priest was still alive.   The guards quickly dispatched him, as they needed the basement for a new group of prisoners to torture to death.

It is an amazing story of love, sacrifice and choice!

We will most likely never face something as gruesome at this, but we can learn from the life of this priest who chose a good attitude in spite of the dire circumstances.
How much smaller do your problems and circumstances seem now?

Choose to have a positive attitude!

Tough Questions:

- Do you have a positive attitude? Are you glass half full or glass half empty?

- Would your family and friends say you had a positive attitude?

- Do circumstances dictate your attitude?

- What is holding you back from having a positive attitude?

- Do you have a better attitude at work than at home? Why?

- What are the triggers that can set you on a path towards a negative attitude?

- How much time do you spend dwelling on the negative outcomes of the past? Why?

- Do you believe a positive attitude is a choice?

Intellectually Curious

Anyone who stops learning is old, whether at twenty or eighty. Anyone who keeps learning stays young. The greatest thing in life is to keep your mind young.
Henry Ford

What does it mean to be intellectually curious? It is a strong desire to know or learn something. It is about a continuous process of learning and acquiring knowledge and wisdom.

It is the desire to invest your time, talents and treasures into knowing how things work, why people do what they do, new concepts and ideas, and or new places to explore. As Henry Ford says above, learning will keep your mind young. Your brain is a muscle and you have to exercise that muscle if you do not want it to atrophy from lack of use.

When I interview people for a job, I always probe for intellectual curiosity. Do they think outside the box? Do they consider different perspectives? What are they doing to improve their knowledge and wisdom? How many books have they read in the last 6 months? What classes or training have they taken to improve their skills?

What is one of the greatest questions in the world, and yet the older we get, we rarely ask this question?

It is the question - WHY!

Who is great at asking WHY? Young children! They are fascinated with the world and how it works. Everything is new and different to them.

They want to explore and when they do not understand, they ask WHY? It can be annoying to those of us with lots of children, and we tend to teach our children to stop asking the questions by giving them vague answers or no answer at all.

Here is another great question asked by those who are intellectually curious:

It is the question - WHY NOT?

This coming week, try asking more of these simple questions – Why? Why Not?

You will be fascinated by the responses you get from people when you ask these simple questions. You can also get to the heart of an issue and determine just how dedicated someone is to their position or idea just by asking these two simple questions.

Questions

- Should we be lifelong learners and intellectually curious?
- Are there benefits to being intellectually curious?
- Can you develop intellectual curiosity?

Should we be lifelong learners and intellectually curious?

When you stop choosing to learn you are basically demonstrating one of two attitudes:

1. Arrogance - I know everything I will ever need to know
2. Ignorance - There nothing new to learn

What I have found is that the more I know and learn, the more I realize how much I do not know!

We know from the Bible and King Solomon, that a prudent person seeks to acquire knowledge but fools only seek folly.   In the book of Proverbs we find that we must engage our heart, our mind and our ears to gain knowledge.   It is a full body experience to gain knowledge and understanding.

Proverbs 1:5

A wise man will hear and increase in learning,
And a man of understanding will acquire wise counsel,

Proverbs 15:14

The mind of the intelligent seeks knowledge,
But the mouth of fools feeds on folly.

Proverbs 18:15

The mind of the prudent acquires knowledge,
And the ear of the wise seeks knowledge.

Proverbs 22:17

Incline your ear and hear the words of the wise,
And apply your mind to my knowledge;

Proverbs 23:12

Apply your heart to discipline
And your ears to words of knowledge.

If you are going to acquire knowledge, then where should you turn to begin this process?

We turn to our heart and mind.   We want to be very circumspect about what we will allow into our hearts and mind and what we want to learn more about. Not everything you read, see or hear will be edifying to you. Therefore seek wisdom and discernment!

Proverbs 4:5-7

Acquire wisdom! Acquire understanding!
Do not forget nor turn away from the words of my mouth.
"Do not forsake her, and she will guard you;
Love her, and she will watch over you.
"The [a]beginning of wisdom is: Acquire wisdom;
And with all your acquiring, get understanding.

You may ask, where does wisdom come from? Wisdom comes from God!
If we ask and seek wisdom, then God will freely give it to us.

James 1:5

But if any of you lacks wisdom, let him ask of God, who gives to all generously and
without reproach, and it will be given to him.

What then is wisdom and discernment? Wisdom and discernment is the
ability to make good decisions! It is the ability to know right from wrong.

If you apply wisdom and discernment to the process with which you
choose to acquire knowledge, then you will be much more likely to gain
knowledge that will be helpful to you and others.

Here are some key things you will want to gain more knowledge about (do
these look familiar?):

- How to exercise and be more physically fit.
- How to be a better friend, spouse, employee, and neighbor.
- How to do a better job of handling money.
- How to have a positive outlook on life.
- How to learn about new things, people and places.
- How to learn more about God, worship, prayer, fellowship and the Bible
- How to be more sympathetic and empathetic.

This list pretty much covers all aspects of your life and is meant to be
comprehensive.   You have to choose which areas are most relevant and
important for your season of life.

As an example, here are some practical things I have learned in the past
few years.

I learned how to do the following:

- Replace brake pads on my car (a close friend taught me)
- Replace the radiator on my daughters car (YouTube video)
- Replace the starter on my son's car (YouTube video)
- How the air war was waged in World War II (book)
- How the Korean was fought (book)
- How to increase influence at work (seminar)
- How to use a chainsaw and cut a tree down (YouTube Video, owner's manual)
- Earned my MBA–Masters of Business Administration (university)

There is still so much more I want to know and learn before I pass from this world and it will take a very intentional effort on my part to find the time, energy and resources to accomplish this task. But I am committed to choosing to increase my knowledge and learning.

What about you? What will you choose to learn this week?

Benefits of Intellectual Curiosity:

- Keeps your mind sharp
- You can save money (by doing your own repairs)
- Increased knowledge - so that you can help yourself and others
- Helps you lead others to a better understanding of the world around them
- Set a good example to your family, spouse and children
- You become more valuable to your employer
- Learning can never be taken from you. It is a lifelong gift

Can you develop intellectual curiosity?

YES! Of course you can.

It may not be easy if this does not come naturally for you, but it is all about the choices you make. You have to choose whether or not you want to know and grow in knowledge.   Here are some of the choices you will have to consider: Who, What, When Where, Why and How

Choices to being Intellectually Curious

- Who or what will you interact with and learn from?
- What will you choose to learn?
- When will you allocate time for learning?
- Where will you do your leaning? Where will you explore?
- Why are you making a particular choice? What is your goal?
- How will you allocate your financial resources towards learning?

Let me give you an example of how I applied these choices.

I love reading and set a goal of reading 12-24 books per year. Here is the process I used this year to find the books I wanted to read this year.

Who

My Pastor, Friends, Bill Gates, my own curiosity about a subject

What

Book recommendations for the people listed above. Bill Gates puts out a list of top books he recommends.   Not all of his recommendations are worth reading, but many of them are pretty good.

My pastor recommended five different books he really enjoyed and would help with my personal growth and education. My friends recommended many different types of book that were all interesting.

Where

Anywhere I have a chance to catch up on my reading. Planes, waiting rooms, hotel rooms, early in the morning, late at night, in the tub (I am in good company here as Winston Churchill and Benjamin Franklin both liked to read in the tub).

When

I read in the early morning and late at night.   On Sunday after church I may take an afternoon to read.   However, I try not to read during the day as this would interfere with job, exercise and family.

Why

I was to stay sharp and learn new and different things. I want to grow personally and professionally and this helps me immensely.

How

I get most of my books from Amazon and almost always buy good used books. I typically spend about $100-$150 for books each year. I do not like e-books yet. I still like to hold a book in my hand, turn the page, mark my place and take notes in the margins.

Here is a list of the books I am reading for 2017 (in no particular order)

- ✓ *Servant on the Edge of History*
- ✓ *T4T: A Discipleship Re-Revolution*
- ✓ *The Sacred Willow*
- ✓ *Half Time*
- ✓ *From Success to Significance*
- ✓ *Private Empire – Exxon/Mobile*
- ✓ *Virtuous Minds*
- ✓ *They Sympathizer*
- ✓ *Courageous Faith*
- ✓ *50 People Every Christian Should Know*
- ✓ *The Seven Decisions*
- ✓ *The Little Things*
- ✓ *The Forgotten 500*
- ✓ *The Myth of the Strong Leader*
- ✓ *Shoe Dog*
- ✓ *Retribution*
- ✓ *Korean War*
- ✓ *Bomber Command*
- ✓ *The Grid*
- ✓ *The Signal in the Noise*
- ✓ *The Travelers Gift*
- ✓ *Vietnam Culture Smart*
- ✓ *The Litigators*
- ✓ *Killing the Rising Sun*
- ✓ *Wise Parenting Principles*
- ✓ *The measure of a Man*

As you can see, the list is quite eclectic. I would not recommend all of these books (I am willing to try a book that is recommended to me, but sometimes they turn out to be disappointing and or offer a viewpoint that I would not advocate to others). However, I do recommend that you become an avid and active reader and learner.

"Rich people have small TVs and big libraries, and poor people have small libraries and big TVs." Zig Ziglar

What will you choose to do? Will you choose to seek wisdom, discernment and knowledge? It is your choice

Tough Questions:

- Are you a curious learner?

- Are you teachable?

- Would you friends and family say you are intellectually curious?

- What is holding you back from being a lifelong learner?

- Are you a know it all?

- What have you intentionally learned in the past 30 days?

- Do you believe learning is a life-long pursuit? If so, what is your plan?

Spiritually Grounded

Do you want to know and better understand your relationship with God? I know I do! Early on I learned there was a "God shaped" hole in my heart. I could try to fill that hole with all the worldly pleasures, but only God could fill that hole.

When I was 14 years old, I first heard the good news of the gospel of Jesus Christ. I was at an evangelical crusade at my high school and I went forward and repented of my sins and accepted Christ as my personal Lord and Savior. This was the first time I had ever head the Good News preached.

It has been almost 40 years since that fateful decision and as I enter the last ¼ of my life, I desire to finish well and I want to have a deeper and more meaningful relationship with God.

As we think about being spiritually grounded it comes down to choices we must make in our life.

Key Choices to being spiritual grounded:

- To pray
- To praise
- To study
- To worship
- To give
- To go & witness

Choose To pray

Prayer is an essential part of every Christian's faith and walk with the Lord. Prayer is like breathing. We need to be continually praying. Pray without ceasing we are told in 1 Thessalonians 5:17. Prayer should continually be on our lips, our hearts and our minds.

Prayer is how communicate with God. Prayer is how we bring our wants, needs and desires to God.

"Don't pray when you feel like it. Have an appointment with the Lord and keep it. A man is powerful on his knees."
Corrie Ten Boom

Prayer is not something that should be done in a hap hazardous way. It can and should be done in an intentional and deliberate way. Now that does not mean there are times when we will cry out to God in the stress and pain of a sudden storm in our life. Certainly we would want to plead and make our petitions know in those desperate times. However, for most of us, those distressing times are few and far between.

Therefore being intentional about your prayer life is critical not only for those who you are praying for, but also for your own relationship with the Lord and daily communion with Him.

The other goal of our prayer life is to be an example for our children and to lead them in paths of righteousness and to teach them how to pray by watching mom and dad praying.

1 Thessalonians 5:16-18

*Rejoice always; **pray without ceasing**; in everything give thanks; for this is God's will for you in Christ Jesus.*

Philippians 4:6

Be anxious for nothing, but in everything by prayer and supplication with thanksgiving let your requests be made known to God.

Choose To Praise

"Prayer and praise are the oars by which a man may row his boat into the deep waters of the knowledge of Christ."
Charles Spurgeon

How do you praise and worship God in times of sorrow, agony, trial and tribulation? Is it even possible to do? What about a storm that literally sweeps your family away?

"Saved alone"
That is the cable that Horatio Spafford received from his wife in November of 1873. The ship she was traveling on with their four daughters collided with another ship and sank. She alone survived the disaster.

The family had been mourning the loss of their son (and brother) and they were taking a trip to Europe to recover from that loss. It was only a last minute business meeting that kept Horatio from joining his family on that fateful voyage.

As he hurried to England to console his grieving wife, he penned the words to an incredible hymn. You can only imagine what was going through his mind as he traveled the same waters that swept away his precious children. He was a man of deep faith and conviction and the words are as fresh today as they were almost 150 years ago.

Take the time to slowly read the words, remember the context and consider the faith of the man who wrote this beautiful and powerful hymn. Let it touch your mind, body and soul.

It Is Well With My Soul

When peace, like a river, attendeth my way,
When sorrows like sea billows roll;
Whatever my lot, Thou hast taught me to say,
It is well, it is well with my soul.

Refrain:

It is well (it is well),
With my soul (with my soul),
It is well, it is well with my soul.

Though Satan should buffet, though trials should come,
Let this blest assurance control,
That Christ hath regarded my helpless estate,
And hath shed His own blood for my soul.

Refrain

My sin, oh the bliss of this glorious thought!
My sin, not in part but the whole,
Is nailed to His cross, and I bear it no more,
Praise the Lord, praise the Lord, O my soul!

Refrain

For me, be it Christ, be it Christ hence to live:
If Jordan above me shall roll,
No pang shall be mine, for in death as in life
Thou wilt whisper Thy peace to my soul.

Refrain

And Lord haste the day, when my faith shall be sight,
The clouds be rolled back as a scroll;
The trump shall resound, and the Lord shall descend,
Even so, it is well with my soul.

Refrain

The loss of a loved one is perhaps the hardest thing to overcome and deal with in our life. To lose all of your children could be devastating and debilitating, but Horatio chose to rise above the grief and sorrow and worship God.

Most of us will never have to deal with something this terrible, but we will all have to deal with trials, troubles and tribulations in our life.

We will all come face to face with that time when we have to make a choice as to whether or not our faith will rocked to its foundation, or if we will CHOOSE to praise and worship God.

The only way to prepare is to seek God's face daily in your own time of study, prayer, praise and worship. Just as an athlete must exercise every day to prepare his mind and body for the competition to come, we must exercise our heart and mind and fill them with God's words and promises. There is no shortcut to preparation.

Choose today to be student of the Bible.

As you continue through this chapter, it is my hope and prayer that you will get a keen sense of the power of praise and worship and realize that God is worthy of our praise – all the time.

Psalm 150:6

Let everything that has breath praise the Lord. Praise the Lord!

Psalm 96:4

For great is the Lord and greatly to be praised;
He is to be feared above all gods.

Choose To study

How much time will you give to study the Bible and memorize God's word?

How much time did you give to: work, sports, hobbies, games, surfing the web, sleeping, eating, and relaxing? None of these are bad things, but the question remains, how much time are you giving God each day?

I found for myself that it is best for me to start each day in prayer, Bible study, reading, writing and contemplation. If I wait until the evening, I am either too tired, or other cares of the world have overtaken my thoughts. I get up an hour earlier than usual to start my day. In the quiet of the morning, before my family starts to stir and work beckons me, I take time to study. It just starts my day off right.

How important is it to hide or treasure God's word in your heart?

The Bible tells us that what proceeds from our mouth is what has come out of our hearts. If we are filling our heart with the Word of God, then hopefully the word of God will proceed from our lips and prove to be edifying and helpful to others (besides building up our own mind and fortifying ourselves).

The Bible tells us we should study the Word so that we may be adequate and equipped for every good work. Every good work would mean as we live and lead our lives each and every day. We do not know what we will encounter; therefore we need to be prepared what whatever comes our way.

2 Timothy 3:16-17

All Scripture is inspired by God and profitable for teaching, for reproof, for correction, for training in righteousness; so that the man of God may be adequate, equipped for every good work.

The psalmist wrote extensively about studying and meditating on God's word. When they used the word meditate in the Bible, it is a much different meaning than how the world uses the word meditate. Today someone will say they are meditating -- meaning they are emptying themselves of all thoughts. To meditate Biblically means to dive into and fill yourself up with God's word and let it permeate you heart, mind, body and soul.

Psalm 119:15-16

I will meditate on Your precepts
And regard Your ways.
I shall delight in Your statutes;
I shall not forget Your word.

Psalm 119:97-98

O how I love Your law!
It is my meditation all the day.
Your commandments make me wiser than my enemies,
For they are ever mine.

Choose To Worship

"Without worship, we go about miserable."
A. W. Tozer

The Bible tells us that David was a man after God's own heart (Act:s 13:22). As such, David was one of the key writers of Psalms. You can find many psalms of praise and worship to God. In the Psalm below you can see how David is choosing to worship God all the time.

Remember, David some pretty tough times. The king tried to kill him, his son rebelled against him, his enemies pursued him and he made some pretty poor moral choices and yet he still choose to praise God all the time.

Psalm 34:1-3

I will bless the Lord at all times;
His praise shall continually be in my mouth.
My soul will make its boast in the Lord;
The humble will hear it and rejoice.
O magnify the Lord with me,
And let us exalt His name together.

Worshipping God is a choice you make each and every day. Worship can be done corporately in a building – such as your church. Many of us would say that we go to Church on Sunday to worship God and offer praise and thanksgiving. Worship can also be done privately in the quiet of your home, in the woods as you walk or as you lie on a distant beach. You are not confined to a time or place to worship. Worship is a choice you have to make each and every day.

We should worship God because He is holy and worthy to be praised. Our God is an awesome God.

Psalm 99:5

Exalt the Lord our God
And worship at His footstool;
Holy is He.

Choose To Give

"We make a living by what we get, but we make a life by what we give."
Winston Churchill

Acts 20:35

... 'It is more blessed to give than to receive.'"

What exactly do I mean by giving? In the context of this chapter I am talking about giving from what I call the trifecta of life:

Time – serving others at the local, national and international level
Talents – using your natural and learned skills to serve others
Treasure – giving and being generous with your money and assets

I like what Proverbs has to say about giving and being generous. Our very nature is one of selfishness and deceit. We are constantly looking out for #`1. We want, what we want, when we want it! The only antidote that I know for selfishness is to be generous. Take the time to honestly evaluate your life and see if you are truly generous in all these areas.

Proverbs 3:9
Honor the Lord from your wealth
And from the first of all your produce;

Proverbs 11:25
The generous man will be prosperous,
And he who waters will himself be watered.

Proverbs 22:9
He who is generous will be blessed,
For he gives some of his food to the poor.

Choose to be generous with your time, talents and treasures and I guarantee you will be blessed – both tangibly and intangibly.

Choose To Go & Witness

Matthew 28:19-20

Go therefore and make disciples of all the nations, baptizing them in the name of the Father and the Son and the Holy Spirit, teaching them to observe all that I commanded you; and lo, I am with you always, even to the end of the age."

GO
MAKE
BAPTIZE
TEACH

This looks like a plan to me! It is simple, concise, specific, and intentional.

Go – in the context of this verse it means – "as you are going". In other words, as you are living your life, have a plan to share the Good News of the Gospel of Jesus Christ. This will require study, prayer, and meditation on God's word. You cannot effectively share what you do not effectively know. Go also means to have a plan to share the Gospel with the whole world

Make – making disciples requires training – you have to train yourself first and be a disciple of Christ. Not just a follower of Christ, but a disciple. To be a disciple means to follow the teacher and serve him exclusively.

Baptize – a public profession of an inward change. It is an act that allows us to be identified in the death, burial and resurrection of Christ. This is an intentional profession of faith in Christ

Teach – to be a teacher, requires a willingness to sacrifice time to prepare and to share how God has changed your life. It means you have to know and more importantly LIVE what you are teaching.

Choose to Go

Let your "yes" be on the table and trust God to guide you. You may only ever go to your neighborhood or city. However, you may also have the opportunity to go further and farther than you ever imagined when you put your YES on the table.

You also need to choose to be intentional. With our children, we have chosen to help them have a biblical worldview by setting a goal to have them serve on a mission trip on every continent of the world before they graduate from high school.

The idea is for them to see God working around the world, in different languages and cultures. We want our children to realize that God is the God of the whole world and not just a God in suburban Atlanta. Too many Christians have a myopic view of the world because they never get out and experience the world and experience God at work around the world.

As Christians, we should want, need and desire to share the Good News of the Gospel of Jesus Christ. To be a "witness" is to tell others about how God has changed your life, priorities and passions since you repented of your sins and put your trust in Jesus as your personal Lord and savior.

2 Corinthians 5:20

Therefore, we are ambassadors for Christ, as though God were making an appeal through us; we beg you on behalf of Christ, be reconciled to God.

1 Peter 3:15

but sanctify Christ as Lord in your hearts, always being ready to make a defense to everyone who asks you to give an account for the hope that is in you, yet with gentleness and reverence;

Mark 13:10

The gospel must first be preached to all the nations.

In addition to these choices, I also believe it is important to have a biblical world view to be spiritually grounded. A biblical world view is one which we as Christians would use to "filter" all situations and circumstances in our life.

A biblical world view is in direct contrast and competition to how most people view the world today. We are told there are many gods or no god at all. We are told there is no moral absolute, but that situational ethics are appropriate. We are told that the world has evolved and there is no creator. To have a biblical world view means you are "swimming upstream" against a deluge of divergent ideas.

Joshua 24:15

"If it is disagreeable in your sight to serve the Lord, choose for yourselves today whom you will serve: whether the gods which your fathers served which were beyond the River, or the gods of the Amorites in whose land you are living; but as for me and my house, we will serve the Lord."

In Joshua's farewell address to his people, he laid out a clear choice for them. Serve the local gods, or serve the LORD. Joshua made it very clear as to his choice. It was an amazing act of leadership and faith.

A biblical word view does not offer you the choice of "playing it safe". You must choose a side! As for me and my house, we will serve the lord!

Biblical World View

1. There is a God (and only one God)
2. Moral Absolutes - Bible – the word of God
3. Revelation – God is revealed in nature
4. Creation – God created everything (not evolution)
5. Jesus is the son of God
6. Value human life
7. Salvation – through grace, by faith, in Christ alone
8. Government and society appointed by God
9. Social action – Share the Good News (witness)
10. Judgment – there will be a final judgment from God

To be clear, this list is not exhaustive, but these are the key principles of a biblical world view.

There is a God (and only one God)

It is clear in the Bible that our God is a jealous God and He does not want, need or desire us to worship any other gods.

 The first of the Ten Commandments tells us that God is to be our only God.   Believing and having faith that there is only ONE God is foundational to all your other beliefs.

The world today will challenge us and tell us there are many different gods and that they are all equal in value and importance.   Today we see people worshipping nature, worshiping false gods, or choosing to worship nothing other than the almighty dollar or even themselves.

Who will you choose to worship? Who will you choose to give honor and glory and praise?

Exodus 20:3

"You shall have no other gods before Me."

Isaiah 45:5

 "I am the Lord, and there is no other;
Besides Me there is no God.

Isaiah 43:10

"You are My witnesses," declares the Lord,
"And My servant whom I have chosen,
So that you may know and believe Me
And understand that I am He.
Before Me there was no God formed,
And there will be none after Me.

Isaiah 44:6

*"Thus says the Lord, the King of Israel and his Redeemer, the Lord of hosts:
'I am the first and I am the last,
And there is no God besides Me.*

Moral Absolutes - Bible – the word of God

The Bible is our guide in life.   It contains everything we need to know about how to live a good and righteous life.   From the Bible we learn how to deal with others, worship and praise God, handle money, manage conflict, encourage, admonish, lead, pray study, teach, view circumstances and so much more.   The Bible is not just another book on our shelf. It is God's gift to us and our instruction guide for life.

Timothy 3:16

All Scripture is inspired by God and profitable for teaching, for reproof, for correction, for training in righteousness;

The Ten Commandments are the moral absolute that become our divining rod for making good choices in life.   In the old testament we are given 10 simple commandments.

Exodus 20:3-17

"You shall have no other gods before Me.

"You shall not make for yourself an idol, or any likeness of what is in heaven above or on the earth beneath or in the water under the earth. You shall not worship them or serve them; for I, the Lord your God, am a jealous God, visiting the iniquity of the fathers on the children, on the third and the fourth generations of those who hate Me, but showing loving kindness to thousands, to those who love Me and keep My commandments.

"You shall not take the name of the Lord your God in vain, for the Lord will not leave him unpunished who takes His name in vain.

"Remember the sabbath day, to keep it holy. Six days you shall labor and do all your work, but the seventh day is a sabbath of the Lord your God; in it you shall not do any work, you or your son or your daughter, your male or your female servant or your cattle or your sojourner who stays with you. For in six days the Lord made the heavens and the earth, the sea and all that is in them, and rested on the seventh day; therefore the Lord blessed the sabbath day and made it holy.

"Honor your father and your mother, that your days may be prolonged in the land which the Lord your God gives you.

"You shall not murder.
"You shall not commit adultery.
"You shall not steal.
"You shall not bear false witness against your neighbor.

"You shall not covet your neighbor's house; you shall not covet your neighbor's wife or his male servant or his female servant or his ox or his donkey or anything that belongs to your neighbor."

I love how Jesus boils down the Ten Commandments into two simple truths. We try so hard to complicate the world we live in and Jesus just cuts through all the clutter and tells us where our heart should focus. We may not be able to memorize the Ten Commandments, but we should surely be able to remember these two below.

Matthew 22:36-40

"Teacher, which is the great commandment in the Law?" And He said to him, "'You shall love the Lord your God with all your heart, and with all your soul, and with all your mind.' This is the great and foremost commandment. The second is like it, 'You shall love your neighbor as yourself.' On these two commandments depend the whole Law and the Prophets."

We have the choice to believe that Bible is our guide in life and the holy inspired word of God. There were 40 or so writers of the bible and it was written over a period of about 1,600 years.

You have to decide (by faith) if you believe the Bible or not. You cannot pick and choose chapters of verses you like and will follow and discard the rest. You have to choose to take the Bible as a whole and not add or delete anything from it.

Revelation – God is revealed in nature

I did not grow up in a religious family or with any biblical education or information.   However I can distinctly remember as a child looking into the heavens and wondering where it ended. How far back did it go? I remember thinking – how did we get here? How can something come from nothing?   I did not know about God or creation, but it was evident even to me as a young child that there was something much bigger than myself in the universe.

I remember a preacher coming to our church and telling us that when missionaries would venture into distant villages and lands, they would invariable find the tribes worshiping something (usually nature) and it was only after they shared the Good News and explained God and creation that the people were able to make the connection in their heart.   Because of what they had seen in nature, they knew they needed to worship something.   It was these missionaries who were able to point them to our Lord and Savior.

Given a choice, will you choose to worship nature or the creator of all nature?

Romans 1:20

For since the creation of the world His invisible attributes, His eternal power and divine nature, have been clearly seen, being understood through what has been made, so that they are without excuse.

Psalm 19:1-4

*The heavens are telling of the glory of God;
And their expanse is declaring the work of His hands.
 Day to day pours forth speech,
And night to night reveals knowledge.
There is no speech, nor are there words;
Their voice is not heard.
Their line has gone out through all the earth,
And their utterances to the end of the world.
In them He has placed a tent for the sun,*

Creation – God created everything

This is always a fun discussion with non-believers. The world has accepted the "Theory of Evolution" hook, line and sinker. Charles Darwin did a great disservice to humanity with his crude observations and conclusions. It takes much more faith to believe in the theory of evolution than it does to believe there is a creator. It really is a matter of faith and what you choose to believe.

They are still looking for the missing link between man and apes and how we evolved. What will you choose to believe?

Genesis 1:1

In the beginning God created the heavens and the earth.

Isaiah 44:24

Thus says the Lord, your Redeemer, and the one who formed you from the womb,

"I, the Lord, am the maker of all things,
Stretching out the heavens by Myself
And spreading out the earth all alone,

Isaiah 45:18

For thus says the Lord, who created the heavens (He is the God who formed the earth and made it, He established it and did not create it a waste place, but formed it to be inhabited),"I am the Lord, and there is none else.

Nehemiah 9:6

"You alone are the Lord.
You have made the heavens,
The heaven of heavens with all their host,
The earth and all that is on it,
The seas and all that is in them.
You give life to all of them
And the heavenly host bows down before You.

Jesus is the son of God

You cannot be a Christian without the firm belief that Jesus is the Son of God. He (Jesus), did not claim to be a teacher or prophet, but he claimed to be the Son of God. The angel told Mary she would give birth to the Son of God. Then God Himself called down from heaven to declare Jesus was His Son, when Jesus was baptized. He also declared it on the mountain when Jesus was transfigured.

The choice is yours! What will you chose to believe?

Luke 1:35

The angel answered and said to her **(Mary)**, *"The Holy Spirit will come upon you, and the power of the Most High will overshadow you; and for that reason the holy Child shall be called the Son of God.*

Matthew 16:15-17

He **(Jesus)** *said to them, "But who do you say that I am?" Simon Peter answered, "You are the Christ, the Son of the living God." And Jesus said to him, "Blessed are you, Simon Barjona, because flesh and blood did not reveal this to you, but My Father who is in heaven.*

Matthew 17:5

While he was still speaking, a bright cloud overshadowed them, and behold, a voice out of the cloud said, "This is My beloved Son, with whom I am well-pleased; listen to Him!"

Matthew 3:17

And behold, a voice out of the heavens said, "This is My beloved Son, in whom I am well-pleased."

John 5:19

Therefore Jesus answered and was saying to them, "Truly, truly, I say to you, the Son can do nothing of Himself, unless it is something He sees the Father doing; for whatever the Father does, these things the Son also does in like manner.

Value human life

We are created in the image of God, He knew us even as he formed us in our mothers' wombs. Human life is precious all the time in all places and environs. . All lives matter to God – today, tomorrow, and forever. In fact, God loves mankind so much, he sent his only Son to die on the cross for all humanity.

In a world where many place no value on human life at all, we are called to value all human life. We should consider that God knows the very number of hairs on our head (although this is easy with me since I am bald), God knows when a sparrow falls to the earth and tells us how much more valuable we are to Him than a sparrow.

Will you choose to value human life and take a stand against evil?

John 3:16

 For God so loved the world, that He gave His only begotten Son, that whoever believes in Him shall not perish, but have eternal life.

Genesis 1:27

God created man in His own image, in the image of God He created him; male and female He created them.

Psalm 139:14

I will give thanks to You, for I am fearfully and wonderfully made; Wonderful are Your works, And my soul knows it very well.

Psalm 139:13

For You formed my inward parts; You wove me in my mother's womb.

Jeremiah 1:5

"Before I formed you in the womb I knew you, And before you were born I consecrated you; I have appointed you a prophet to the nations."

Matthew 10:29-31

Are not two sparrows sold for a cent? And yet not one of them will fall to the ground apart from your Father. But the very hairs of your head are all numbered. So do not fear; you are more valuable than many sparrows.

Romans 8:31-32

What then shall we say to these things? If God is for us, who is against us? He who did not spare His own Son, but delivered Him over for us all, how will He not also with Him freely give us all things?

Salvation – through grace, by faith, in Christ alone

Jesus left no room for speculation in terms of salvation. He tells us that no one will come to God but through Him. There is no equivocation, no hesitation, and no negotiation. The Cross has the final word with the death, burial and resurrection of Christ.

Each of us has to choose at some point in our life to put our faith and trust in Jesus Christ alone for our salvation. What will you choose? Where do you place your faith?

Ephesians 2:8-9

For by grace you have been saved through faith; and [a]that not of yourselves, it is the gift of God; not as a result of works, so that no one may boast.

John 14:6

Jesus *said to him, "I am the way, and the truth, and the life; no one comes to the Father but through Me.

Romans 10:9-10

that if you confess with your mouth Jesus as Lord, and believe in your heart that God raised Him from the dead, you will be saved; for with the heart a person believes, resulting in righteousness, and with the mouth he confesses, resulting in salvation.

Government and society appointed by God

Render unto Caesar the things that are Caesars and to God the things that are God's. Jesus spoke these words to those who tried to trip Him up on the question of whether to pay taxes or not. We are called to be in subjection to the legal authorities and to be good citizen.

However, this does not mean we mindlessly obey the government. We are never called to do things that would violate our faith and beliefs. The best saying I have heard along these lines is this:

It is never wrong to do right and it is never right to do wrong. That may sound pithy, but it is a simple truth.

Consider Daniel who refused to stop praying to God and was thrown in the lion's den. Or Shadrach, Meshach, and Abednego who refused to bow to a statue of the king as if he were a god, and were thrown into the fiery furnace. They refused to obey the legal authority because it was against their faith and belief.

So, we should pay our taxes, obey the speed limit, vote, serve on jury duty, and chose to be good citizens. At the same time we should also know where the line is to be drawn and chose to only serve our God when necessary (regardless of the earthy consequences). Perhaps in our lifetime we will never face this choice, but as for me and my house, we will serve the Lord.

What will you choose to do? Will you choose to be a good citizen? Will you render to God what is God's and to Caesar what is Caesar's? The choice is yours.

Romans 13:1-2

Every person is to be in subjection to the governing authorities. For there is no authority except from God, and those which exist are established by God. Therefore whoever resists authority has opposed the ordinance of God; and they who have opposed will receive condemnation upon themselves,

1 Peter 2:13-17

Submit yourselves for the Lord's sake to every human institution, whether to a king as the one in authority, or to governors as sent by him for the punishment of evildoers and the praise of those who do right. For such is the will of God that by doing right you may silence the ignorance of foolish men. Act as free men, and do not use your freedom as a covering for evil, but use it as bond slaves of God. Honor all people, love the brotherhood, fear God, and honor the king.

Social action – Share the Good News

Matthew 28:19-20

Go therefore and make disciples of all the nations, baptizing them in the name of the Father and the Son and the Holy Spirit, teaching them to observe all that I commanded you; and lo, I am with you always, even to the end of the age."

This famous verse from the book of Matthew has literally launched thousands of Christians into the mission field. It is a call to action and a choice we all have to make.

You can choose to start preparing yourself by memorizing the Romans Road to salvation. It is a simple way to share with others the plan of salvation God has for all of us.

Romans Road

Do you know God's grace and mercy? Follow the "Romans Road" and see how God has laid out his plan of salvation for your life:

Romans 3:23

for all have sinned and fall short of the glory of God.

We must all realize that we are sinners and that we need forgiveness. We are not worthy of God's grace.

Romans 6:23

For the wages of sin is death, but the gift of God is eternal life in Christ Jesus our Lord.

If we remain sinners, we will die. However, if we accept Jesus as our Lord and Savior, and repent of our sins, we will have eternal life

Romans 5:8

But God demonstrates His own love toward us, in that while we were still sinners, Christ died for us.

Through Jesus, God gave us a way to be saved from our sins. God showed us His love by giving us the potential for life through the death of His Son, Jesus Christ.

Romans 10:9-10

that if you confess with your mouth the Lord Jesus and believe in your heart that God has raised Him from the dead, you will be saved. For with the heart one believes unto righteousness, and with the mouth confession is made unto salvation

Just confess that Jesus Christ is Lord and believe in your heart that God raised Him from the dead and you will be saved!

Romans 10:13

For "whoever calls on the name of the LORD shall be saved."

There are no religious formulas or rituals -- Call upon the name of the Lord and you will be saved!

Romans 10:17

So then faith comes by hearing, and hearing by the word of God.

God's plan of salvation is simple and free.   There is nothing you can do to "earn" it.   You only need to believe and confess.   Do not think your sins are too great to be forgiven.   Christ died for ALL sin and there is nothing so bad that you have done, that Christ cannot forgive you.

I followed this path of salvation in many years ago as a teenager and my life has never been the same. I pray you will follow this path to God's love and forgiveness.

Judgment – there will be a final judgment

There is a final reconciliation that will take place in heaven one day. Are you ready? We find in the bible the following about the final judgment:

- Every person is appointed to die once and then be judged
- Christ will be the judge
- Everyone will appear before the judgment seat
- There is a book of life with all the written deeds (both good and bad)
- Those whose name are not in the book of life will be throw into the lake of fire

Revelation 20:11-15

Then I saw a great white throne and Him who sat upon it, from whose presence earth and heaven fled away, and no place was found for them. And I saw the dead, the great and the small, standing before the throne, and books were opened; and another book was opened, which is the book of life; and the dead were judged from the things which were written in the books, according to their deeds. And the sea gave up the dead which were in it, and death and Hades gave up the dead which were in them; and they were judged, every one of them according to their deeds. Then death and Hades were thrown into the lake of fire. This is the second death, the lake of fire. And if anyone's name was not found written in the book of life, he was thrown into the lake of fire.

Hebrews 9:27

And inasmuch as it is appointed for men to die once and after this comes judgment,

2 Corinthians 5:10

For we must all appear before the judgment seat of Christ, so that each one may be recompensed for his deeds in the body, according to what he has done, whether good or bad.

Tough Questions

- Are you spiritually grounded?
- If not, what will it take to become spiritually grounded?
- Do you study enough?
- Do you pray enough?
- Do you give enough?
- Do you serve enough?
- Do you know what you believe? Are you prepared to defend your faith?
- Will you choose to – GO, MAKE, BAPTIZE and TEACH?

Emotionally Sensitive

"Nobody cares how much you know, until they know how much you care." Theodore Roosevelt

Do you know someone who is tone deaf? Have you ever heard them try to sing a song? It is one of the most painful things you can experience in life. It makes you cringe and want to crawl under a rock to escape the noise coming out of their mouth. The sad part is many people who are tone deaf have no idea just how bad they are at singing. Fortunately for society, there are not that many tone deaf people.

How about this question: Are you emotionally tone deaf?

What does it mean to be emotionally tone deaf? It means you are not able to be compassionate, sympathetic or empathetic to those around you. You do not notice (or choose not to notice) pain, joy, suffering, fear, sadness or anger. Your heart is hardened to the point of callousness.

I know that there have been times in my life when I have been emotionally tone deaf. I was not the least bit sensitive to the feelings of others and was only concerned with my own thoughts, emotions, wants, needs and desires. It was selfishness of the highest order!

This was especially true when I was under pressure or stressed. Today, I have learned to be more thoughtful and quiet in these situations.

I took a test at work called Hermann Brain Dominance, and without boring you with the details, it told me that I was mostly "whole brained", meaning I was equally, analytical, practical, relational, and experimental.

Most people have a high dominance in one of these areas (thus the name of the study). However, one of the things it pointed out to me was that when I was under stress, I lost almost all of my relational dominance and went into analytical and practical mode. What this meant was I lost my ability to be sympathetic or empathetic and focused only on the task or goal.

I was surprised by the finding, but when I was honest with myself, I knew the test was accurate and true. Since then I have strived to make the choice to be sympathetic where necessary and empathetic where possible and not let my circumstances or stress dictate my actions.

I am still a work in process!

Sympathy vs. Empathy

I have always been confused about the difference between sympathy and empathy. So I wanted to clarify and hopefully offer some simple explanation to describe the differences.

I saw a great cartoon that illustrated the difference between sympathy and empathy. In the cartoon, one bear is crying and the other bear says " I am so sorry for your pain". This is sympathy. In the next pane, it shows the same two bears and they are both crying. This is empathy.

Sympathy = I care about your suffering

Empathy = I feel your suffering

When you are empathetic, you connect with the person because most likely you have had a similar circumstance in your life.

When we lost our third child to a miscarriage if was a devastating blow to our family. We received many sympathy cards and calls from friends and family. However, it was my Bride's friends who had experienced the same pain and loss that came beside us and showed empathy and compassion during that difficult time. To be clear, both the sympathy and empathy were warmly welcomed and received and needed.

I had a close friend of mine offer a sympathy card and it was very kind of him to do so. However, several years later, they experienced their own tragedy when his wife miscarried twins.   It was a very difficult situation. I was able to offer both empathy and sympathy to my dear friend because of what we had gone through ourselves.

A few months later he called me to apologize for only offering me sympathy when we had experience our miscarriage. He was actually very tearful for only sending a card and not reaching out. I put his heart at ease and told him he was not able to be empathetic as that point because he had not experienced that situation. You see, he now realized how painful it was for us and wanted me to know how much he loved our family and felt our pain.   It was a very endearing phone call indeed!

Have you ever considered that the storms, trials and tribulations that you encounter and overcome, will allow you to be empathetic to others if you allow yourself to be open and vulnerable to share.

The Bible actually teaches us about our suffering and how it is not always for our own edification, but for helping others who will go through similar circumstances.

<u>2 Corinthians 1:3-4</u>

Blessed be the God and Father of our Lord Jesus Christ, the Father of mercies and God of all comfort, who comforts us in all our affliction so that we will be able to comfort those who are in any affliction with the comfort with which we ourselves are comforted by God.

So what does it mean to be emotionally sensitive to others?

It means to be compassionate, sympathetic or empathetic towards others. It means to be on the lookout for situations and opportunities to encourage, offer hope, and love others in times of distress, challenges, trials and tribulations.   It also means to rejoice in victories and celebrate the good times.

When I think about compassion I think about several different Bible characters that showed compassion and in some instances mercy and grace as well.

- Father of the Prodigal Son – when his son was still far off he had compassion for him.
- Good Samaritan - when he saw the wounded traveler, he had compassion for him.
- King – felt compassion for slave that owed him 10,000 talents (60 million days 'worth of work) 1 Talent = 16 years of wages.   An impossible sum for anyone to pay back.
- Jesus – felt compassion for many different people - the leper, the blind man, for the hungry crowd who followed him, for the mother whose son died.   These were both physical needs as well as emotional needs.

Let's look more closely at the story of the Good Samaritan.   It is a story many have heard, but perhaps you did not know all of the historical context and the characters in the story.   Let's read the story below:

Luke 10:25-37

And a lawyer stood up and put Him to the test, saying, "Teacher, what shall I do to inherit eternal life?" And He said to him, "What is written in the Law? How does it read to you?" And he answered, "You shall love the Lord your God with all your heart, and with all your soul, and with all your strength, and with all your mind; and your neighbor as yourself." And He said to him, "You have answered correctly; do this and you will live." But wishing to justify himself, he said to Jesus, "And who is my neighbor?"

Jesus replied and said, "A man was going down from Jerusalem to Jericho, and fell among robbers, and they stripped him and beat him, and went away leaving him half dead.   And by chance a priest was going down on that road, and when he saw him, he passed by on the other side.   Likewise a Levite also, when he came to the place and saw him, passed by on the other side.   But a Samaritan, who was on a journey, came upon him; and when he saw him, he felt compassion, and came to him and bandaged up his wounds, pouring oil and wine on them; and he put him on his own beast, and brought him to an inn and took care of him.   On the next day he took out two denarii and gave them to the innkeeper and said, 'Take care of him; and whatever more you spend, when I return I will repay you.' Which of these three do you think proved to be a neighbor to the man who fell into the robbers' hands?"   And he said, "The one who showed mercy toward him."   Then Jesus said to him, "Go and do the same."

So in this story we have three key players; the Priest, the Levite and the Good Samaritan.

Now to better understand, you have to realize that the Samaritans were a half-breed people that no respectable Jewish person would have contact with.   On the other hand, the Priest and the Levite would be some of most respectable people in Jewish society. They would have known the law (to love the neighbor as themselves) and more importantly, given their position in society, they should have been the most compassionate, loving and merciful.

The priests were held in very high regard and all priests came from the Levites (but not all Levites were priests). The Levites were called to be "set apart" and actually served in the tabernacle and helped the priests.

Jesus is using the extreme contrast in characters to show us that it is not enough to know the law or be respected or respectable, it is the choices and actions which are important.

The Samaritan chooses to stop and show compassion and mercy.   He may or may not have known the law, but he did know enough to stop and help a stranger.

Question

- Should we be emotionally sensitive to others?

I hope you said "YES" to that question.

Why? Because our God is a compassionate God.

 In Exodus 34 we see God describing his own character to Moses and He calls Himself compassionate.   In Psalms 116 we see the Psalmist calling out God's character and proclaiming our God is compassionate. In 2 Corinthians we see God called out as comforting us in our affliction.

If we are indeed made in the image of God, then we should want to have the same characteristics of God and one of those key characteristics is compassion.

Exodus 34:5-6

The Lord descended in the cloud and stood there with him as he called upon the name of the Lord. Then the Lord passed by in front of him and proclaimed, "The Lord, the Lord God, compassionate and gracious, slow to anger, and abounding in loving kindness and truth;

Psalm 116:5

Gracious is the Lord, and righteous;
Yes, our God is compassionate.

In the verses below you will see a call to action for us as believers in terms of how we should deal with all of the different emotional situations we will encounter. These are words of action!

- Encourage one another
- Bear one another's burdens
- Rejoice
- Weep
- Edify
- Forgive

Thessalonians 5:11

Therefore encourage one another and build up one another, just as you also are doing.

Galatians 6:2

Bear one another's burdens, and thereby fulfill the law of Christ.

Romans 12:15

Rejoice with those who rejoice, and weep with those who weep

Ephesians 4:29

Let no unwholesome word proceed from your mouth, but only such a word as is good for edification according to the need of the moment, so that it will give grace to those who hear.

Colossians 3:12-14

So, as those who have been chosen of God, holy and beloved, put on a heart of compassion, kindness, humility, gentleness and patience; bearing with one another, and forgiving each other, whoever has a complaint against anyone; just as the Lord forgave you, so also should you. Beyond all these things put on love, which is the perfect bond of unity.

Why do we do this? Because we are one body in Christ.   When one member of the body suffers, we all suffer. When one member of the body rejoices we all rejoice.

1 Corinthians 12:25-26

so that there may be no division in the body, but that the members may have the same care for one another. And if one member suffers, all the members suffer with it; if one member is honored, all the members rejoice with it.

As with all things we have talked about in this book, you have the choice as to whether or not you will be emotionally sensitive.   In order to be emotionally sensitive, you will have to open you heart and be more vulnerable that you have been in the past.

It also means opening yourself up for potential disappointment, hurt and pain.   However, these are a small price to pay when you can have such a positive effect on many people.

Remember, your choice to be emotionally sensitive, extends beyond the four walls of you home. It extends to your neighborhood, your community, your church, your work place and even to strangers.

Choices:

- Choose To listen
- Choose To have compassion/empathy/concern
- Choose To have sympathy/understanding/consideration
- Choose To act when the opportunity presents itself
- Choose not to look the other way and ignore others
- Choose to be vulnerable and share your past experience

Tough Questions:

- Are you genuinely concerned with the feelings and emotions of others?
- Would your friends and family say you are compassionate, empathetic and or sympathetic?
- Are you empathic where applicable or sympathetic where necessary? Or are you apathetic, cynical or have a hard heart?
- When was the last time you showed compassion?
- Do you believe compassion is a strength or a weakness?
- What can you do today to become more sensitive?

Two Questions Again

I told you we would be coming back to these questions at the end of the book. So here we are at the end and you are probably wondering why I had you answer these questions to begin with. Now I can tell you.

As I have talked to numerous people about these concepts, the overriding concern is time and money. People want to know how they will find the time and money to be effective in all these areas when they are already in a busy world where budgets and time are stretched thin.

We all have the same amount of time each day. It does not matter if you are rich, poor, fat, skinny, white, black, plumber, preacher, physician or pilot. We all have 24 hours in each day. How we CHOOSE to use that time is what will allow us to achieve all of our goals and objectives.

It is not easy managing your time or treasures and it is not really a lot of fun either. However, if you are intentional about how you CHOOSE to use your time and treasures, then I believe you will start to see significant progress against these seven key areas of your life.

Where will you find that time and money? Look back on your answers to those two questions I asked and you will see that you probably have the ability to better manage these two areas, such that you can be more intentional.

In case you did not do the exercise at the beginning of the book, I have included the questions again here for you to answer. Please be truthful and thoughtful with your responses. Nobody but you is ever going to read them anyway.

Take some time and don't rush through this.

1. On average, how many hours do you spend in front of a screen each week (for pleasure not work)

   - TV/Cable/Satellite
   - Phone/Tablet
   - Computer
   - Gaming, Web Surfing, Social Media, Movies, etc.

Write your answer here: Avg. # of hours = _____

2. On average, and how much did you spend each month on the following?

   - Fast Food (Chick-fil-a, McDonalds)
   - Coffee/Beverage (Starbucks, Dunkin Donuts)
   - Casual Dining or Fine (Applebee's, Outback)
   - Hobbies?
   - Movies, gaming, sports?
   - Payments for Deprecating assets – boats, RV's, ATV's, motorcycles, snowmobiles, etc.

Write your answer here: Avg. amount spent = _____

Can you honestly say you are not capable of finding some extra time and money?

Choose today to be more thoughtful and intentional about how you spend your time and treasures and you will find out just how much more you can accomplish.

Recap

Here are all the key choices and tough questions for each chapter in one place. The Seven key choices I asked you to make at the beginning of the book:

1. Will you choose to be physically fit?
2. Will you choose to be more engaged in your most important relationships?
3. Will you choose to lead an economically sound life?
4. Will you choose to be mentally positive?
5. Will you chose to be intellectually curious?
6. Will you choose to be spiritually grounded?
7. Will you choose to emotionally sensitive?

Physically FIT

- Would your family and friends say you were physically fit?
- Do you think you are physically fit?
- If you are not physically fit – why not?
- What is holding you back? Is it time, mental, physical, emotional, or financial reasons that are holding you back? Are these real obstacles?

Relationally ENGAGED

- Are you fully engaged with the most important relationships in your life?
- If not, why not? What is holding you back?
- Would your family and friends say you were fully engaged?
- Which relationship is hardest for you? Why?
- How hard are you willing to work to restore a relationship?

134

Economically SOUND

- Are you a good steward of your financial resources?
- Would your family and friends say you are a good steward?
- Does your bank statement say you are a good steward?
- Are you saving more?
- Are you spending less?
- Can you be more generous?
- Do you have a budget and follow it?
- Do you serve money and possessions or do they serve you?
- What is the toughest area of your finances to control?
- If you are married, are you aligned on spending, saving, giving, generosity and goals? If not, why not?

Mentally POSITIVE

- Do you have a positive attitude? Are you glass half full or glass half empty?
- Would your family and friends say you had a positive attitude?
- Do circumstances dictate you attitude?
- What is holding you back from having a positive attitude?
- Do you have a better attitude at work than at home? Why?
- What are the triggers that can set you on a path towards a negative attitude?
- How much time do you spend dwelling on the negative outcomes of the past? Why?
- Do you believe a positive attitude is a choice?

Intellectually CURIOUS

- Are you a curious learner?
- Are you a know it all?
- Are you teachable?
- Would you friends and family say you are intellectually curious?
- What is holding you back from being a lifelong learner?
- What have you intentionally learned in the past 30 days?
- Do you believe learning is a life-long pursuit? If so, what is your plan?

Spiritually GROUNDED

- Are you spiritually grounded?
- If not, what will it take to become spiritually grounded?
- Do you study enough?
- Do you pray enough?
- Do you give enough?
- Do you serve enough?
- Do you know what you believe? Are you prepared to defend your faith?
- Will you choose to – GO, MAKE, BAPTIZE and TEACH?

Emotionally SENSITIVE

- Are you genuinely concerned with the feelings and emotions of others?
- Would your friends and family say you are compassionate, empathetic and or sympathetic?
- Are you empathic where applicable or sympathetic where necessary? Or are you apathetic, cynical or have a hard heart?
- When was the last time you showed compassion?
- Do you believe compassion is a strength or a weakness?
- What can you do today to become more sensitive?

Final Thoughts

First, thank you so much for taking the time to read this book. It is my prayer that this has been a blessing to you and your family.

Secondly, if you have an opportunity to send me an e-mail with your thoughts, comments or suggestions, that would be very helpful.

Finally, I hope you were encouraged and strengthened by what you read.

paulbeersdorf@gmail.com

Blessings to you and your family!

Paul Beersdorf

Study Group Lessons

It was my desire to include an 8 week study guide for groups who wanted to dig a little deeper together and share some of their thoughts, ideas and perhaps even provide some accountability.

Please use these weekly lesson plans as a starting point for choosing to make positive changes in your life. While they are designed to be used as a group, you can also go through this by yourself as well.

Remember, you will only get as much out of these lessons as you put into them. Please choose to be open, honest and willing to listen to the thoughts and comments from others.

The idea is to read a chapter each week and then come prepared to answer the questions as a group. Most of the questions are not designed to be easy. Expect to be challenged and to be forced to think about your answers.

Lesson 1
Choices

Scripture Memory Verse:

<u>Proverbs 3:5-6</u>

Trust in the Lord with all your heart
And do not lean on your own understanding.
In all your ways acknowledge Him,
And He will make your paths straight.

Q. – Why did you choose to read this book?

Q. – What were the key points you got out of this chapter?

Q. – Do you believe the choices you make define who and what you are and or will become?   Explain your answer

Q. – Of the seven key areas of your life – which is currently offering the most difficult choices?   Why are the choices so difficult?

Physically
Relationally
Economically
Mentally
Intellectually
Spiritually
Emotionally

Q. – In which of these key areas can you make some quick choices that will have an immediate positive effect on your life?

Q. – What are some positive choices you can make this week to start changing your trajectory?

Q. – Why does God allow us to make choices?

Q. – Do you believe this statement?– "to choose not to choose is to choose". What does this mean?

Q. – How much time do you spend worrying about circumstances outside your control?

Next Steps

Determine to have a plan this week to make better choices (regardless of the circumstance).

Things to consider for making better choices:

- Prepare by praying
- Reading the bible (start by reading a chapter of Proverbs each day)
- Seek Wise Counsel
- Try not to make critical choices if you are Hungry, Angry, Lonely or Tired – this creates the acronym H.A.L.T.   Halt or stop before you make a poor choice
- Guard what goes into your eyes, ears, heart, mouth and mind

140

Lesson 2
Physically Fit

Scripture Memory Verse:

1 Corinthians 6:19-20

Or do you not know that your body is a temple of the Holy Spirit who is in you, whom you have from God and that you are not your own for you have been bought with a price: therefore glorify God in your body.

Q. – What were the key points you got out of this chapter?

Q. – Do you believe it is important to be physically fit? If not, why not?

Q. – What does it mean when the Bible says our body is temple?

Q. – Why would God want you to be physical fit?

Q. – What is preventing you from being physically fit?

Q. – How can this group help you to be more physically fit?

Q. – Are you willing to modify your diet, change your eating habits, start an exercise routine and choose to be physically fit?

Next Steps

Determine to have a plan this week to be more physically fit. Check with your doctor before beginning a new fitness routine

Who is going to hold you accountable for being physically fit?

Lesson 3
Relationally Engaged

Scripture Memory Verse:

<u>John 13:34</u>

A new commandment I give to you, that you love one another, even as I have loved you, that you also love one another.

Q. – What were the key points you got out of this chapter?

Q. – Which relationships do you struggle with the most? Why?

Q. – Which relationships are in need of more time and energy?

Q. – How does forgiveness play an important role in relationships?

Q. – Is it ok to ignore some relationships?

Q. – What is the most important relationship in your life? Why?

Q. – Do you hold others to expectations that you don't have for yourself?

Q. – Does God desire us to be relationally engaged? Explain.

Next Steps

Make a list of all your most important relationships (by name) and pray diligently for each and every one of them daily for a week.

Reach out to someone with whom you need to reconnect and work on repairing/restoring that relationship.

Lesson 4
Economically Sound

Scripture Memory Verse:

Matthew 6:24

No one can serve two masters; for either he will hate the one and love the other, or he will be devoted to one and despise the other. You cannot serve God and wealth.

Q. – What were the key points you got out of this chapter?

Q. – How difficult is it to live within a budget? Why?

Q. – How important is self-discipline when it comes to financial matters? Why?

Q. – How much stuff do you have that you really don't need?

Q. – How much is enough?

Q. –Are you prepared from an unexpected financial expense?

Q. – Are you buried in debt? Why? What lead to the debt?

Next Steps

Go to Dave Ramsey website for resources and tools to help you.

Create a budget for the month and live within that budget. Only pay cash (debit card) and do not use credit.   If you have already done this, then set a new savings and or giving goal for the month and see if you can achieve that goal.

Lesson 5
Mentally Positive

Scripture Memory Verse:

<u>Philippians 4:11</u>

Not that I speak from want, for I have learned to be content in whatever circumstances I am

Q. – What were the key points you got out of this chapter?

Q. – Are you content? If not, why not?

Q. – What circumstances typically trigger a bad attitude for you?

Q. – Do you believe your attitude is 100% within your control? If not, who/what is responsible?

Q. – Do the people you primarily hang out with have good attitudes or bad attitudes? Do you need a new set of people to hang out with?

Q. – Read chapter 4 of Philippians and know that Paul was in Chains when he wrote this. How did he respond to contentment?

Next Steps

Read, study and meditate on the entire book of Philippians this week. Take good notes and read commentaries as well.

Memorize this saying:

"I cannot always control my circumstances, but I can always control my response"

Lesson 6
Intellectually Curious

Scripture Memory Verse:

<u>Proverbs 1:5</u>

A wise man will hear and increase in learning,
And a man of understanding will acquire wise counsel,

Q. – What were the key points you got out of this chapter?

Q. – Are you a lifelong learner? What does this mean to you?

Q. – Do you believe it is important to continuously be learning? Why?

Q. – How can being intellectually curious help you in these areas?
- Family
- Job
- Church
- Community

Q. – Who do you go to for wise counsel? Why?

Q. – What is the difference between wisdom and knowledge? Where does real wisdom come from (hint: answer is in the bible)?

Next Steps

Read at least one new book this week (something you have never read before). Or learn one new skill this week.

Read the entire book of proverbs over the course of one month (there are 31 chapters).

Lesson 7
Spiritually Grounded

Scripture Memory Verse:

<u>1 Thessalonians 5:16-18</u>

Rejoice always; pray without ceasing; in everything give thanks; for this is God's will for you in Christ Jesus.

Q. – What were the key points you got out of this chapter?

Q. – Are you spiritually grounded? What evidence would you offer?

Q. – Do you have a biblical world view? Why is this important?

Q. – Are you prepared to defend your faith? How would you do that?

Q. – How much time do you devote each week to spiritual matters (prayer, study, worship, praise, etc.)? Is this enough? What more could you be doing?

Q. – Is God more interested in you knowing His commands or being obedient and doing His commands? Why?

Next Steps

Memorize all the verses of the "Romans Road" as a starting point. Study and pray over each verse to gain a clear understanding of how they all tie together.

If you do not have one – purchase a prayer journal and commit to pray for others on a regular basis (including yourself)

Lesson 8
Emotionally Sensitive

Scripture Memory Verse:

2 Corinthians 1:3-4

Blessed be the God and Father of our Lord Jesus Christ, the Father of mercies and God of all comfort, who comforts us in all our affliction so that we will be able to comfort those who are in any affliction with the comfort with which we ourselves are comforted by God.

Q. – What were the key points you got out of this chapter?

Q. – What is the difference between sympathy and empathy? Which is more important?

Q. – Are you sensitive to the emotions of others? If not, why not?

Q. – How good are your listening skills? How can you become a better listener?

Q. – Do you believe compassion is a key attribute a Christian should have in their life? Why? Explain.

Q. – Why is wisdom and discernment so important when applying compassion?

Next Steps

Work on your listening skills this week and ask clarifying questions when you do not understand. Pray for a sensitive heart and a willingness to be more compassionate.

Made in the USA
Columbia, SC
28 January 2018